Paisa Vasool? Not Quite.

A COMMON MAN'S GUIDE TO MONEY, REAL LIFE, AND FINANCIAL CLARITY

HARSH SONI

This is a work of nonfiction. The events and the incidents mentioned in the book are true and real. However, some names and characteristics have been changed, some events have been compressed, and some dialogues have been recreated.

First Edition: July 2026
Printed in India

Printed at: Gapmeta Ventures Pvt. Ltd., Navi Mumbai
Typeset in EB Garamond

ISBN: 978-93-6070-052-2

Cover Design: Priya Vora

STORYMIRROR
Stories that reflect you

Publisher:	StoryMirror Infotech Pvt. Ltd. Unit No-F/705, 7th Floor, Kailas Corporate Lounge, Veer Savarkar Road, Vikhroli Park Site, Vikhroli West, Mumbai-400079, Maharashtra, India.
Web:	storymirror.com
Facebook:	@storymirror
Twitter:	@story_mirror
Instagram:	@storymirror
Email:	marketing@storymirror.com

This book is dedicated to my wife, Nilisha – who has been my rock through every one of these mistakes, and the quiet, smarter half of almost every decision I eventually got right.

None of this – not the career, not the kids, not the courage to walk out and chase NYVO – would have been possible without you.

TABLE OF CONTENTS

PREFACE

Hi, I'm Harsh.

If we'd met in 2009, I'd have introduced myself as a fresh-faced 22-year-old MBA grad with a head full of Wall Street fantasies and a wardrobe full of ill-fitting blazers. If we'd met around 2022, I'd have probably been somewhere between a flight, a roadshow, and an IPO (Initial Public Offering) listing party – with about 50 IPOs behind me, a passable handshake, and the tired eyes of someone who has read one too many red herring prospectuses. And today, I'm the founder of NYVO Money, trying to fix the way Indians think about money before they make the same 15 mistakes I did.

That last part is what this book is about.

This book is for the Indian household that earns decently, saves something, owns too many products, and still does not know if it is truly okay.

But before we get there, a quick origin story – because the choices that put me in front of you started long before I knew anything about finance.

I was not a great student. I scraped through till the 10th, found my legs in commerce, and somehow ended up doing a B.Com and then an MBA. I finished the MBA before I turned 22. On my 22nd birthday – April 2009 – I got my first job. Looks neat on paper. Looks almost intentional.

It wasn't.

The honest reason I rushed through my MBA was a girl. I liked her. I was terrified that if I dawdled even one extra year, she'd get married off and I'd be left holding a half-finished thesis and a broken heart. So I sprinted. Cleared the MBA. Got the job. And then – spoiler alert – did not marry the girl. Life is funny like that.

Around the same time in 2008, I had picked up a book called Den of Thieves by James B. Stewart. If you haven't read it, it's a thrilling deep-dive into the dirty underbelly of Wall Street in the 1980s. I read it the way other 20-year-olds read Harry Potter. By the last page, I had decided I was going to be an investment banker. Not a banker. An investment banker. There's a difference, and at 21, I was very particular about that difference.

Then I graduated in 2009.

2009 was the year after Lehman crash, and the investment banking offer letters I'd been daydreaming about weren't coming. I started at IDBI Bank in commercial banking in Indore, on a princely salary of ₹18,000 a month. Six months later I got my break at SBI Caps(Mumbai); eventually I made it to Kotak Investment Banking and Bank of America. Thirteen years, fifty-odd IPOs (including IPOs of DMart, Zomato, Delhivery, Nykaa), thirty-plus M&As, Institutional Placements, Rights Issue and what not, and a final bonus that – for a kid who'd started at ₹18,000 – was a number I could not have imagined.

Not bad for a guy who only joined an MBA because of a girl.

And then, one fine day, I walked away from all of it.

I joined slice – a fintech that, at the time, was one of the hottest names in the country. The timing was poetic. Almost immediately after I joined, the regulations changed, the entire business model came under fire. I didn't run from it -rebuilt working alongside the founder, I can say this that I helped slice navigate the long, unglamorous journey from being a fintech to becoming a proper commercial bank – one of the more interesting transformations the Indian financial system has seen in recent years.

Somewhere in the middle of all that, something started to bother me.

I was sitting in rooms where decisions were being made about how millions of Indians borrow, save, and spend. I'd built a career advising the largest companies in the country on how to handle their money. And yet, when I looked at my own life – the bike I never bought, the stocks I never should have touched, the EMIs and the FOMO investments and the tax-saving products I'd bought because someone said, "Sir, last date hai (It's the last date)" – I realised something deeply uncomfortable.

I had been making the same kind of mistakes that millions of Indian families are making. Different zeros, same mistakes.

And the more I looked at the Indian financial landscape, the worse it got. Financial products being mis-sold by people who didn't understand them, to people who needed them most. Insurance dressed up as investment. Investment dressed up as savings. Savings eaten alive by inflation. A whole industry that, for all its glass towers and conference rooms, was failing the one person it was supposed to serve – the regular, hard-working Indian household.

That realisation became NYVO Money.

NYVO Money is my attempt – our attempt – to actually help Indians learn money. Not sell them another product. Not give them another tip. Just slow down, look at the mistakes most of us make, and help them avoid the ones that hurt the most. This book is part of that mission. It's the long version of a conversation I wish someone had had with me when I was 16 and had ₹34,000 in my pocket.

So that's the rough shape of the life behind this book. Investment Banker. CFO (Chief Financial Officer). Founder. Husband, father, occasional idiot with money. About a hundred small pages of confessions ahead of you.

These aren't the mistakes of someone who didn't know money. These are the mistakes of someone who should have known better – who studied finance, sold finance, raised money, advised on billions of dollars of capital, and still managed to fumble his own personal finances in 15 different ways. If anything, that's the point of this book. Knowing the theory of money and being good with your own money are two completely different sports.

I'm hoping you'll laugh a little, wince a little, and walk away with a few quiet "Oh god, I do that too" moments. If even one of these chapters saves you from one of these mistakes, I'd consider this book paisa vasool.

The title, by the way, is the first joke. Because looking back at most of these decisions – Paisa vasool? Not quite.

Let's begin.

CHAPTER

01

How I Lost ₹25,000 Before I Could Grow a Moustache

Every great financial story begins with a brash teenager. This one is no different.

I was somewhere between Class 10 and Class 12, around 2002 to 2004, and second-hand mobile phones were having their golden age in India. Everyone wanted a Nokia 1100 or Nokia 2100. Almost no one could afford a new one. So if you knew where to find a good used handset, where to clean it up a bit, and how to talk to people, there was money to be made. And somehow, between school bags and tuition classes, I figured out I knew how to do all three.

Over the next year and a half, I bought and sold second-hand phones the way other kids in my class collected WWE trading cards. Nothing fancy – just a small, scrappy, very offline little hustle. By the end of it, I had stitched together close to ₹34,000.

You have to remember what ₹34,000 was in 2004 to a kid in school. It wasn't money. It was a *fortune*. It was a brand-new bike with my name on it. It was the kind of independence that, when you're 16, feels like the difference between being a child and being an adult.

I should have bought the bike.

I did not buy the bike.

Because somewhere around the same time, I'd gotten interested in the stock market. I had read about it. I had watched it on TV. I had, with all the wisdom of a teenager who had once finished a chapter on financial accounting, decided that I had figured the markets out. So I took every last rupee of my hard-earned ₹34,000 – every phone deal, every haggling session, every "bhaiya, last price kya hai" – and I put it into the stock market.

Not into a mutual fund. Not into a few different stocks.

Into two stocks.

Two.

And then came May 2004.

For those who weren't around or weren't watching: 17 May 2004 was one of the worst days the Indian stock market has ever had. The election results came in, the new government wasn't the one the markets had bet on, and the Sensex fell off a cliff. Circuits were hit. Trading was halted. Twice. People who had been in the market for decades were stunned. I, all of 16 or 17, with two stocks and the entire weight of my mobile-phone empire riding on them, just stared.

By the time the dust settled, my ₹34,000 was about ₹9,000.

I had lost roughly ₹25,000 due to the events of a single afternoon.

I sat with that number for a long time. I didn't know what to say. I didn't know who to tell. I had, in the most spectacular way possible, lit my own bike on fire.

A few weeks later, when I finally had to admit it, I went to my father and asked him to buy me the bike I had been planning to buy myself. He did. He's a kind man. But there was a particular kind of quiet in that ride home – me on the new bike, him on his – that I think is its own little chapter in my education.

What did I learn?

A lot, eventually. But the cleanest, simplest lesson – the one I've watched smart adults forget over and over again in the 20+ years since – is this:

Never put everything you have into one or two of anything.

It doesn't matter if it's two stocks. It doesn't matter if it's one company's ESOPs (Employee Stock Ownership Plan). It doesn't matter if it's that one "sure-shot" tip your cousin's friend gave you at a wedding. Concentration looks like conviction when things are going well. It looks like devastation the day they aren't.

The market doesn't care that you're 17 and saved up for a bike. It doesn't care that you worked weekends. It doesn't care about your story at all. It will take a bad afternoon and turn it into a very long evening.

The good news is that ₹25,000 is, in the grand scheme of a life, a relatively cheap tuition fee for a lesson this important. Some people pay this lesson in lakhs. Some pay it in crores. I got off lightly.

I just didn't get the bike.

Mistake #1, logged.

Fourteen more to go.

CHAPTER

02

The Cute Little Credit Card That Cost Me ₹1 Lakh

Every Indian boy in an MBA hostel has, at some point, been handed a piece of plastic he was not emotionally ready for. This is the story of mine.

The year was 2008. I was in the second year of my MBA in Bombay, living in a hostel where the mess somehow did not include food. Don't ask me how a hostel mess in 2008 didn't include food. I think the explanation, when we asked, was a long and confident sentence that ended with *"...so basically you boys figure it out."* We figured it out.

My monthly budget looked something like this:

- Rent and hostel fees: paid for, thank God.
- Pocket money from home: ₹5,000.

- Petrol and "other expenses": ₹2,000 of that.
- Breakfast, lunch, and dinner – every day, for a 21-year-old, in Bombay – on the remaining ₹3,000.

Reader, that math has never made sense. It still doesn't.

Then ICICI Bank came along like Santa Claus on a quarterly target. The bank arrived on campus, asked us to submit our college IDs, and a few weeks later, every single MBA student in our batch was holding a fresh credit card. Not a real, grown-up credit card. A small, cute, "starter" card with a tiny limit. The kind of card that, if it could speak, would have said, *"Hi, I'm just here for the experience."*

I was very, very happy. I had no income. I had no payslip. I had a college ID, a hostel address, and a hunger problem. And now I had a credit card.

What could possibly go wrong?

For the first few months, I behaved. The bill came; I paid the full amount. The bill came; I paid the full amount. I felt very mature about it. I would casually flick the card out at the petrol pump and at the dosa joint and at the occasional movie, and I would think, *this is what being an adult feels like.* It feels like swiping plastic without checking the balance. Magnificent.

Then the cash got tight one month. I turned to the bottom of my credit card bill, where there was a friendly little number called the "Minimum Amount Due."

Minimum amount due are three of the most expensive words in personal finance. They sound like a discount. They sound like flexibility. They are, in fact, a slow-motion noose with a polite font.

I paid the minimum. I told myself I'd settle the rest next month. Next month came. I paid the minimum again. Next month came; I paid the minimum again. The bank had no objections. The bank, in fact, was *delighted*. The bank loves a man who pays the minimum.

By this point I had finished my MBA, started my first job at IDBI Bank, and assumed that having a real salary would naturally fix this problem. It did not. A real salary just gave me a higher minimum payment to make. The credit card bill, like a brash teenager, kept growing. Every month I added a little more. Every month the amount piled up a little more.

Eighteen months in, I finally added it all up.

₹1,00,000.

One lakh rupees. On a card that had felt, in 2008, like Monopoly money. On purchases that, individually, had each felt small enough to ignore. There was no big extravagant moment. There was no Goa trip with a private yacht. There was no impulse-buy of a watch I couldn't afford. There was just *a thousand here, two thousand there, dinner with friends, fuel, a new shirt for an interview, a pair of headphones, drinks one night, a movie ticket the next* – for a year and a half.

That is the polite, terrifying truth about credit card debt: it does not arrive in one big mistake. It arrives in 800 small, perfectly explainable ones.

I sat in front of that statement for a while. ₹1 lakh in 2009, to a guy on a starter banking salary, was not just money – it was months of work. There was no way I could clear it from my next paycheck, or even the one after that. So I did the only thing left to do.

I took a personal loan.

I – a man who had just spent five years studying finance, who would within a few months be helping companies raise capital – went to a bank, took out a high-interest personal loan, and used it to pay off a higher-interest credit card. I had, in other words, taken on debt to clear debt. The full circle was complete. I was no longer the arrogant kid with a starter card. I was now a junior banker with an EMI he didn't talk about.

The one-line rule I now live by: *if you cannot pay the full bill at the end of the month, you cannot afford whatever you bought.*

Everything else about credit cards – the minimum amount due, the 40% interest, the slow accumulation of *"yeh toh chhota hi hai, scene nahi hai"* repeated three hundred times – is just the punishment for forgetting that single sentence. There is one part of credit card debt nobody warns you about: it is not the public mistake. It is the quiet mistake. The one Indian families don't talk about because it carries a particular kind of shame. Friends don't disclose it. Spouses sometimes don't disclose it. Parents almost never do. So the spiral compounds in private, with no second pair of eyes to interrupt it.

Today, the irony is not lost on me. I now run a money company designed, in part, to give 21-year-olds the boring, unflashy, "just-look-at-the-number" view that 21-year-old me would have ignored anyway. But maybe – just maybe – today's 21-year-old, with a real-time view of his money on his phone, won't.

Mistake #2, logged. Thirteen more to go.

CHAPTER

03

How I Sold My Mutual Funds – and Then Blamed the Mutual Funds

When I joined investment banking, my salary jumped from ₹18,000 to ₹32,000.

In 2010-rupees, that felt like getting drafted to the NBA. Suddenly, after months of carefully rationing every chai and every auto, I had what felt like *an actual budget*. I could afford rent. I could afford food. I could afford the occasional dinner that didn't end in regret. And – most thrillingly – I could afford to invest. Like a real grown-up. With a little brown leather wallet of my own.

So I started saving. Small amounts, but consistently. ₹500 here, ₹1,000 there, every month, into the stock market and, soon after, into mutual fund SIPs. This was 2011-2012. KYC was a physical form. NACH mandates were a physical form. To start a single SIP, you had to fill out a piece of paper, sign it, attach a cancelled cheque, and *post the whole thing somewhere*. I felt very smart while doing all of this.

I should not have felt smart.

Because the very first thing I did – the foundation of everything that came next – was wrong.

I picked mutual funds the way most Indians picked mutual funds in 2011, and the way far too many of us still do today: I sorted by past returns, scrolled to the top, and put my money in whatever had performed best in the last three years.

That was it. That was the entire investment process.

I did not ask:

- Why am I investing this money?
- When will I need it?
- What kind of fund matches that time horizon?
- What's the risk profile?
- Am I okay watching this go down 30% in a bad year?

No. I asked one question – *which fund went up the most last time?* – and then I bought it. Because last time's winner had to be next time's winner, right? This was, in fact, the famous and clearly-stated opposite of how every mutual fund disclosure ever printed has told us to behave. I had read every disclosure. I had ignored every disclosure. *Past performance is not indicative of future results,* the SEBI line said. Cool, cool, cool, I thought, scrolling further down the past-performance table.

Most of what came up at the top of those lists were small-cap and mid-cap funds – which, fair enough, had been on a tear. I started SIPs (Systematic Investment Plans) into them and felt very accomplished. Every month, ₹1,000 went out of my account into a small-cap fund. I did not look at the portfolio. I did not need to. I was, after all, investing for *the long term*, baby.

Or so I thought.

Eighteen months later, in 2012-13, my parents and I started talking about buying a house in our hometown. I had a bonus, plus the savings I'd been quietly stacking up. I needed a down payment. I opened my mutual fund portfolio for the first time in a long time, expecting to see the gentle magic of compounding.

The portfolio was almost exactly what I had put in.

A year and a half of disciplined SIPs. ₹500 here, ₹1,000 there. Through every market wobble. And the result was a number that looked, give or take a rounding error, like the sum of my contributions. Flat. Static. *Boring*.

I was furious.

What kind of scam was this? What kind of system was this? I had heard so much about mutual funds. People had told me about this magical thing called compounding. And here I was, eighteen months in, with a portfolio that looked like a fixed deposit's slightly less responsible cousin. So I did what any disappointed, mildly indignant young investor does – I yanked the money out, used it for the house, and then, just to make my point to the universe, *I stopped investing in mutual funds altogether for the next year and a half.*

Take that, mutual funds.

(Bonus fact, which I learned only later: that flat 2011-13 stretch was followed by one of the more meaningful Indian small and mid-cap rallies in recent memory. The very funds I had sold in disgust did very, very nicely after I left the table. I had managed, in eighteen months, to buy at the wrong time, sell at the wrong time, and stop investing right before things got interesting. A grand slam.)

Years later, I went back and looked at it properly. Calmly. With the unhelpful clarity of hindsight.

And the embarrassing truth jumped out:

The mutual funds had not failed me. I had failed the mutual funds.

I had bought *small-cap and mid-cap* funds – high-volatility, long-horizon products – and I had given them an eighteen-month leash. That is, financially, like buying a banyan tree sapling and getting upset that it isn't shading your driveway by the second monsoon. Small caps need years. Mid caps need years. They need to be allowed to go through one bad cycle, sometimes two, before they reward you. I had given them barely one rough patch and walked out muttering about scams.

But the deeper mistake was not even the fund choice. The deeper mistake was that I had no goal.

I had not asked myself, before clicking "Start SIP," what this money was actually for. If I had – if I had said *"this money is for a house down payment in two years"* – I would have known instantly that small caps were the wrong instrument. That money belonged in something boring and short-duration. Something liquid. Something that wasn't going to trip on its own shoelaces a week before I needed the cash.

But I hadn't done any of that. I had just looked at past returns and bought the shiniest one.

What did I learn?

First: *invest with a goal, not a tab*. Money for a wedding next year does not belong in the same fund as money for retirement in thirty years. They are different timelines, and they need different vehicles. The single most important question before starting any SIP is, when will I need this money? If you cannot answer it in years, you have not finished the homework.

Second: *past returns are a starting point, not a strategy*. They tell you which funds were in fashion last season. They tell you nothing about which funds will be in fashion next. Indian markets, in particular, rotate categories – large caps, mid caps, small caps, sectoral, thematic – in cycles long enough to make every retail investor exactly one cycle late. By the time a small-cap fund is at the top of the past-returns list for three straight years, you are usually buying it just before its rough patch begins.

Third: *if a portfolio is "static" for eighteen months, that is not a problem with the portfolio. That is the cost of admission.* The whole reason equity gives you the long-term return it does is precisely because it does not deliver that return in a smooth line. If you can't sit through a flat or down period, you don't get the long-term return. That is the deal. Nobody is sneaking it past you in the small print – the small print is exactly that.

I lost about a year and a half of compounding because I'd started with the wrong question. And I came within six months of never buying a mutual fund again – which, in a 30-year working life, would have been the most expensive sulk of my career.

Mistake #3, logged. Twelve more to go.

CHAPTER

04

I Got ESOPs Three Times. I Understood Them Zero Times

Here is a thing that should embarrass me more than it does: I spent thirteen years in investment banking – building IPO models, walking founders through option pools, explaining ESOP grants to other people's employees on diligence calls – and I, personally, *did not understand my own ESOPs,* until embarrassingly recently.

I have been granted ESOPs three times in my career.

Once at Kotak Investment Banking. Once at Bank of America. Once at slice.

Three different structures. Three different tax styles. Three different "wait, what?" moments. Let me walk you through each one, mostly so you don't repeat my version of any of them.

Grant 1: Kotak – and the day I felt rich for about an hour

Kotak's ESOPs, in my time, were granted at something close to a market-linked price. Not free. Not face value. There was a base price, plus some option-value premium baked in. You got the right to *buy* shares from the company at this strike, after a vesting period.

When my first tranche vested, I did the only thing my excited 29-year-old brain could think to do: I exercised, in full, immediately. The market was a bit higher than the strike. On paper, my "profit" looked like ₹3–4 lakh. Which, for a guy who is in early stages of his career, was real, life-altering money.

Except -- and this is the part the headline number hides - there was no "credit" arriving. I first had to *pay* the exercise price out of pocket, and pay the perquisite tax (salary-slab) up front via my employer. The net cash I actually saw, after both tax outflows, was around ₹2 lakh.

I sat there, at my desk, looking at the bank SMS, and went through the seven stages of grief in roughly four minutes.

What had happened was the classic Indian ESOP rookie sequence:

- **Exercise price** – I had to pay the strike price to actually convert options into shares. That's real money out of my pocket, on the day of exercise. Nobody had explained this in capital letters. The grant document had explained it in normal letters.
- **Perquisite tax** – On the day of exercise, the difference between fair market value and the strike price is treated as *salary income*. Not capital gains. Salary. Taxed at your slab

rate. For me, sitting in the highest bracket, that's roughly a third of the "gain" lopped off before I had even sold a single share.

- **What was left (and the capital gains tax I then owed)** – after exercise outflow plus perquisite tax, I had about ₹2 lakh of net cash. And because I sold the shares at exercise, the residual gain was taxed *again* as short-term capital gains (STCG) - another hit on top of the perquisite tax. This was the biggest mistake. I could have or should have held those shares.

I learned, in that single SMS, that the headline number on an ESOP screen is essentially marketing copy. The actual takeaway is whatever survives a two-step tax gauntlet.

Grant 2: Bank of America – the easy one

Bank of America gave me RSUs, not options. Restricted Stock Units. The simplest of the three structures. This is the same structure of ESOPs that all MNC company employees get in India.

There's no exercise price. The RSU just vests into a share at the prevailing market price. On vesting, the bank automatically sells a chunk to cover the perquisite tax – typically ~30% in my case – and the rest credits to my US brokerage account as cash-equivalent shares I can sell whenever I want.

If you've never had RSUs and someone is offering you a choice between RSUs and normal options at the same headline number, take RSUs. Every time. They're cleaner, they don't require you to put up exercise capital, and you can't accidentally forget to exercise them and watch them expire (which, by the way, happens more often than people admit).

Grant 3: slice – the long, slow private bet

At slice, the ESOPs were granted at face value – basically, the strike was the share's nominal value, not its current valuation. Big upside if the company went up. slice was, and is, a private company. So these are still locked up, illiquid, and waiting for a liquidity event that may or may not come on a timeline I'd like.

I'm holding them. I'm hopeful. I'll let future-Harsh write the next chapter on how that worked out. (If you're reading this and the answer is "it did," you can stop reading here. If it didn't, see Chapter 17, where I quietly rebrand them as a "long-duration option.")

A tiny, useful crash course on Indian ESOP tax (the part I wish someone had handed me at 24)

ESOPs in India are taxed at two events. Both events bite separately, and forgetting either one is how people end up with surprise tax bills:

1. **At exercise – perquisite tax.** Fair Market Value on exercise date minus exercise price, taxed as perquisite income. The employer typically deducts this via TDS or you must pay upfront.

2. **At sale – capital gains tax.** Sale price minus Fair Market Value on the date of exercise. This is taxed depending on holding period and whether the shares are listed.

Holding-period rules, roughly:

- **Listed shares** held for *more than 12 months* → Long-term capital gains, taxed at 12.5% (on gains above ₹1.25 lakh per year, post Budget 2024).

- **Listed shares** held for *less than 12 months* → Short-term, 20%.
- **Unlisted shares** (most startups, including slice) held for more than 24 months → Long-term, 12.5% without indexation.
- **Unlisted shares** held for *less than 24 months* → Short-term, at slab rate.

There is one happy carve-out worth knowing: if your employer is a DPIIT-recognised eligible startup, the perquisite tax on exercise can be deferred by up to five years from exercise (or until you sell the shares, or 14 days after you leave the company – whichever comes first). This was introduced specifically because employees of cash-poor startups were getting hit with massive perquisite tax bills on illiquid shares they couldn't sell. If your startup qualifies, ask HR. Most don't volunteer this.

And the question almost nobody asks before signing the offer letter

Here is the single most important ESOP question, and almost no one asks it at the offer stage:

If I leave the company, how long do I have to exercise my vested options?

Most Indian startups I have seen – and I have seen many – give you 60 to 90 days. Sometimes less.

That sounds reasonable until you sit in it. You leave a job. You're switching cities, dealing with notice periods, tax filings, maybe a baby, maybe a pivot. You have ₹15 lakh of vested options, and to convert them you need to write a cheque to your former employer for the exercise price plus pay perquisite tax on the spread out of your own pocket, on shares that are *unlisted and illiquid* and may stay that way for years. All in 90 days.

Most people, when they actually run this math, don't exercise. The options expire. Years of vesting, gone, because of an exercise window nobody flagged at the offer stage.

Some companies have started offering 5 or 10-year post-exit exercise windows. A few have even set up structures to lend the exercise capital. Ask. If the answer is 90 days, ask if it can be extended – many companies may do it, it just takes a board approval.

What did I learn?

First: *the headline ESOP number on your offer letter is marketing.* The real number is what you take home after exercise price, perquisite tax, and capital gains tax. That number is sometimes 30–40% lower than the marketing one. Build your decision on the real number.

Second: *RSUs > options at the same headline value, almost always.* Cleaner, no exercise capital, no expiry surprise. If you have a choice, take the cleaner instrument.

Third: *the post-termination exercise window is the most important clause in the entire ESOP document, and it is buried on page 14.* Read it before you sign. Renegotiate it before you sign.

Fourth, the meta-lesson: *don't outsource understanding of your own compensation.* If you can't, on a single A4 page, sketch the cash flows of your own ESOP grant – what you pay, what you owe, when you owe it, what you take home – you don't actually have ESOPs. You have a coupon for a future tax filing problem.

I had ESOPs three times. I worked in finance the whole time. And I still managed to be naive at every grant. So if you're holding an offer letter right now with "₹X crore in ESOPs" written on it in a friendly green font – pause. Open a calculator. Find a CA or write to me. Ask the four questions above. Then sign.

Mistake #4, logged. Eleven more to go.

CHAPTER

05

I Bought Bitcoin at $85. I Still Managed to Lose Money

This is, on paper, the most embarrassing chapter in this book.

In 2013, I bought Bitcoin at $85.

Yes. Eighty. Five. Dollars. A coin.

Stop reading for a second. Open your phone. Check the price. Now come back. We will both pretend that didn't just happen.

I have always been an obsessive reader of weird tech corners – forums, blogs, the kind of obscure stuff you went looking for in 2013 when the internet still felt like a back-alley library. Somewhere in that browsing, in early 2013, I came across a long, slightly conspiratorial post about a thing called Bitcoin. A digital currency. No central bank. Mined on computers. I read about it for a week.

Then I went on a Singapore-based exchange – I don't even remember the name now, which tells you everything about how much due diligence I did – and I bought one Bitcoin at $85.

I felt like a *visionary*.

I told two friends. Both said, in slightly different words, that I had bought magic internet money and was a moron. I held it for roughly a year. The price went up. I sold, in 2014, at $350.

Quadruple my money in about a year. I closed the laptop. I told my wife. I think I said the words, "I am a stud."

I did not buy Bitcoin again.

Read that line again. *I bought Bitcoin in 2013 at $85, sold for a 4x in 2014, and never bought it again*. In the universe of financial mistakes, "had the entire generation-defining trade in his hands and walked away" is a very specific kind of pain. Like a tennis player who serves an ace and then quits to become an accountant.

For about five years after that, I did nothing. Investment banking work was crushing. I was at Kotak, then Bank of America. At some point, internal embargoes came in across the Indian investment banks - most stock trading needed pre-clearance and minimum hold periods. At Bank of America, the rules got stricter still - I couldn't even hold any stocks unless they were pre-existing. We were allowed mutual funds and that was about it. So whatever instinct I had to pick anything individually was now actively forbidden by my own employment contract.

Then 2019 happened, and I, having forgotten the entire lesson of the previous chapter of my own life, decided I was, once again, a stud.

Crypto was back in the news. Doge, Polygon, Ethereum, things ending in -inu. Friends were quitting jobs to "work in web3." Twitter had become an ICO (Initial Coin Offering) showroom. And inside my own head, a very seductive sentence took up residence:

"I had Bitcoin at $85. Imagine what I can do now."

I put in ₹10 lakh. Spread it across the usual suspects (fortunately or unfortunately there was no embargo in investment banks for investing in crypto).

In thirty to forty days, the portfolio went to ₹12 lakh.

I felt, again, like a stud. I started doing what every overconfident retail crypto investor in the history of crypto has done – managing the position. Booking small profits. Rotating. "Taking some off the table." Moving things between coins for reasons I now cannot reconstruct because they were not reasons. They were vibes.

Then a brutal work cycle hit. We're talking 17–18-hour days. IB-grade work. The kind of stretch where your wife stops asking when you'll be home and just starts saying "okay" to whatever you mumble at 1 a.m.

I forgot about the crypto.

Not in a good, "set it and forget it" passive investor way. In a "completely lose track of an asset class that moves 10% before breakfast" way.

When I checked back, the market had cracked. ₹10 lakh had become ₹7 lakh.

This is the part where, if you've ever been here, you know the next move was inevitable.

I did the classic thing. I told myself I would now "manage it actively, rebook, redeploy, recover." I traded. I rotated. I read more Twitter. I made calls based on graphs. The graphs, to be clear, did not care.

When I finally exited, ₹7 lakh had become ₹2.5 lakh.

Total damage: ₹7.5 lakh. Gone. To, depending on which coin we're talking about, a Shiba Inu meme, a Discord server, or just the void.

Let me steelman crypto, because this is not a chapter about crypto being bad.

Crypto is, for a certain kind of investor – one who actually understands custody, on-chain mechanics, project tokenomics, network effects, and is okay losing every rupee they put in – a legitimate alternative asset. People I respect have made and held real money in it. I am not here to tell you it is gambling for everybody.

I am here to tell you it was gambling for me.

Because here is the embarrassing fact, the one I avoided admitting for almost two years: I had no thesis. I could not have told you, with a straight face, why Polygon was undervalued versus Ethereum. I did not understand the difference between a Layer 1 and a Layer 2. I had never read a single project's whitepaper end-to-end. My investment process was: read tweet, feel FOMO (Fear of Missing Out), click buy.

I would not let anyone touch my IPO models with that level of rigour. But I was happy to let my own savings be allocated by the same brain that was, at 1 a.m., scrolling reels.

I had taken every excuse – "I had Bitcoin in 2013," "I work in finance," "I'm not a normal retail investor" – and used them as a substitute for actual homework. The market, very patiently, charged me ₹7.5 lakh for that substitution.

What I'd do today

If a 25-year-old version of me walked into my office tomorrow saying, "Sir, crypto is back, what should I do," this is what I'd say:

- *Decide the size first, the asset second.* Take 1–2% of your portfolio. Label it *casino money* in your own head. Promise yourself you will not add more, no matter what.
- *Don't open a leveraged position.* Ever. You don't have an information edge. Leverage just makes the eventual loss arrive faster.
- *Don't run a 24/7 asset alongside a 14-hour day job.* If you can't watch it daily, you can't own it. Pick a passive vehicle [an index of crypto, an ETF (Exchange Traded Fund) where allowed] or skip the category entirely.
- *Write down, in one paragraph, why this asset will go up.* If you can't, you don't have a thesis. You have a tweet.

And the one sentence I keep coming back to, the one that would have saved me ₹7.5 lakh if I'd believed it: every *"I'm different" sentence you tell yourself before an investment is a flashing red light.* "I had Bitcoin at $85, so I'm different." "I work in finance, so I'm different." If you have to convince yourself the rules don't apply to you, the rules are about to apply to you. Hard.

If you don't understand it, don't invest. If you still want exposure, get a real advisor. Or – and I say this as a slightly bitter exinvestment-banker who has lost money to a Shiba meme – instead at least go to Goa. Sit at the blackjack table. Lose the same money. You'll have a much better time.

Mistake #5, logged. Ten more to go.

CHAPTER

06

I Insured My Phone Before I Insured Myself

For the first ten years of my career, I did not have personal health insurance.

Let me say that again, slowly, to let it land: for the first ten years of a career in finance – at SBI Caps, then Kotak – I, a man who spent every working day talking about risk and downside protection on behalf of companies, did not have a single rupee of personal health insurance.

I am not proud of this. But I am also not surprised by it, because it's exactly what most Indians do.

The reason is the most boring sentence in personal finance: I had health cover from my employer. Decent corporate cover. It paid for my daughter's birth in 2019 without a hitch. It covered the routine doctor visits, the random fevers, the once-a-year, *"Oh god what is this rash"*, panic. As long as I had a job, I had cover. So I never bothered to buy a personal policy.

You can probably already see the shape of the mistake.

My wife, Nilisha – much smarter than me on this stuff – kept saying it. *"We should have a personal policy. Not just the corporate one. What if you change jobs? What if you get sick between jobs? What if something comes up that they don't cover?"*

And I, with the calm wisdom of a man who had successfully not been hit by a bus, would say, *"Arre, but we already have it through the company, no? Why duplicate?"*

She was right. I was wrong. I am a slow learner, and this is documented in many, many chapters of this book.

It eventually took a friend, not my wife, for the message to land. (Husbands of the world: I know. I'm sorry.) Over beer one day, this friend laid it out for me in three sentences. *Corporate cover ends the day you leave the company. Personal cover follows you for life. The longer you wait, the more expensive it gets – and the more "pre-existing conditions" the insurer can hide behind. Buy it now. Buy it now. Buy it now.*

I went home that day and finally bought a policy. I was 32.

The first version of it, embarrassingly, was a ₹10 lakh floater I picked off the internet in an afternoon. The next year, after I'd actually spoken to a proper advisor, I upgraded it to a far better-structured policy. Even "doing the right thing late" can have a sub-version one that is also wrong.

The premium was a punch in the gut.

For me, my wife, and my daughter – a family floater of ₹10 lakh – I was paying around ₹25,000 a year. That number, on its own, isn't insane. What stings is what comes next. If I had bought the same policy at 22, when I started working, the premium would have been a small fraction of that. Ten years of waiting periods would already be done. No "pre-existing conditions" to worry about. A clean health history locked in. Health insurance is one of the very few products in life where being young is genuinely a financial advantage. I had wasted ten years of that advantage by getting it for free through my employer and never thinking to also lock in something of my own.

The good news, at least, was that the policy I bought has been a quiet, beautiful machine for the last several years. With cumulative bonuses for not claiming, that ₹10 lakh cover has grown to roughly ₹75 lakh today. Same premium. More cover. That is what loyalty to a personal health policy looks like – and it is exactly the part you forfeit every time you shop around for a 5% cheaper premium.

Then I tried to do the right thing for my mother.

She was 57. I went to buy her a policy.

I have made many financial mistakes in my life. I have lost money in markets. I have over-leveraged. I have bought things I didn't need with money I didn't have. But nothing – *nothing* – prepared me for the price of buying health insurance for an Indian woman in her late fifties, *for the first time.*

The premium was around ₹40,000, with immediate cover. Per year. For a base cover that, frankly, was just okay. Throw in a battery of medical tests, a few "we'd like to wait two years on this and that" exclusions, and the math became brutal. Over the next decade, I would end up paying multiples of what I would have paid if I had simply bought it for her ten or fifteen years earlier – back when nobody in the family was even thinking about it.

Health insurance pricing is not a gentle slope. It is a cliff. You can stand at the top of it for a long time. The moment you step off, the price drops on top of you.

The good news is that, eventually, I learned. When my son was born in 2024, I wasn't taking any chances. Many Indian health policies require a minimum waiting period - often around 91 days - before a newborn can be added to a parent's policy (the exact rule varies by insurer and product, so check yours). For the policy I had, that meant day 91. The day he was born, I put a reminder in my calendar for day 92. Day 92 came; the next morning, he was on the policy. That is, possibly, the single most efficient piece of life admin I have ever done. My wife was, at last, briefly impressed.

What did I learn?

First, *corporate insurance is not a substitute for personal insurance.* It is a perk that ends the day you stop being useful to your employer. If you are between jobs, on a sabbatical, taking a year off, or – like me now – running your own thing, the corporate cover is gone. The personal cover is what's left.

Second, *the best time to buy health insurance is the moment you have a salary; the second-best time is right now.* Premiums for a 24-year-old are tiny. Premiums for a 32-year-old are okay. Premiums for a 55-year-old are an event. There is no scenario in which waiting is cheaper.

Third, *health insurance is the one financial product nobody on either side wants you to use.* You don't want to claim it. The insurer doesn't want you to claim it. And yet, the day you actually need it, it is the only product on this list that can save you from selling a house, breaking an investment, or borrowing money you'll spend years paying back.

It is the safety net under your entire financial life. Buy the safety net. Buy it before you need it. Buy it for your parents. Buy it for your kids. Add the kid on day 92. Set the calendar reminder.

I sleep better today knowing my family is covered – which matters more now than ever, because today I am building a startup, not collecting a corporate salary. Every entrepreneur secretly knows this: the day you decide to chase your dream is the day a comprehensive personal health policy stops being a *nice-to-have* and quietly becomes oxygen.

Mistake #6, logged. Nine more to go.

CHAPTER

07

The Term Insurance I Bought Because the Bank Asked Me To

The reason I own a flat in Mumbai is because of a society secretary in Andheri.

This is, I have come to learn, a deeply Mumbai sentence, and I would like the rest of India to take a moment to pity us.

In 2018, I was renting in a building in Andheri. I was about to shift from one flat to another flat *in the same society* – barely 30 metres of physical movement, the kind of move where the packers don't really pack, they just pick stuff up and walk it across. Easy. Cheap. Unremarkable.

Except for the secretary.

For non-Mumbaikars: the housing society secretary is, in the Mumbai social hierarchy, somewhere between a bureaucrat, a watchman, and a small-town magistrate. And a *newly minted* society secretary – somebody who has just been elected to the post – is the most dangerous of all, because he has not yet been worn down by the universe and still believes the bylaws are real.

Our newly minted secretary intercepted the move. Loudly. He shouted at me. He shouted at my mother. He invoked rules nobody had ever told us about, written down, or, frankly, made up. He stopped the shifting cold. There was, of course, no actual rule. There was just a man who had recently discovered he had power over other people, and was practising.

We apologised, eventually. We finished the move, eventually. And by the time I closed the door of the new flat that night, I had decided one thing, very clearly:

I am buying my own house. I am never living somewhere a 60-year-old man with a clipboard can yell at my mother again.

I booked a flat in September 2018. Got possession in February 2019. Shifted in April. The Andheri secretary, somewhere in his eternal kingdom, deserves a thank-you note he will never get.

That, however, is not the mistake of this chapter. That part is the setup.

The mistake is what happened the day I went to take the home loan.

The Bundled Pitch

I went to an NBFC (Non Banking Financial Company) home-loan provider – not the one that eventually held my loan; that's a different chapter – and started the paperwork. Somewhere between the salary slips and the property documents, the loan officer slid a brochure across the table.

"Sir, with this loan, we'd recommend you take our credit life insurance. Two-crore cover. One-time premium of about two lakhs. We'll add it to your loan amount, so you don't have to pay anything upfront. Your EMI goes up by about ₹1,600 a month. And – bonus – if you take it, we waive 0.1% of the processing fee."

That last sentence is the cleverest piece of bait in Indian retail finance, and I bit it like a hungry dog.

I said yes. The ₹2L premium got added to my loan principal. My EMI went up by about ₹1,600. I walked out feeling like I had simultaneously secured my family's future, saved on processing fees, and demonstrated mature, responsible adult behaviour. Three for the price of one.

It was, in fact, three mistakes for the price of one.

What I Actually Bought (and What It Actually Cost)

Let me give you the math, because this is the math nobody runs at the loan-signing desk.

The premium: ₹2,00,000.

Industry economics: On bank-pushed credit life insurance, the distributor commission can be anywhere from 40% to 60% of the first-year premium. A meaningful chunk of that ₹2 lakh – possibly ₹80,000 to ₹1.2 lakh – never reached the insurance company at all. It went to the NBFC as commission. I had, without realising it, just paid for the NBFC's books, not my family's protection.

The financing cost: Because the premium was added to the loan, I now owed an extra ₹2 lakh at 8.5% interest, spread over 20 years. Every EMI for the next two decades would have carried a slice of interest on insurance.

I actually prepaid the loan in February 2022, so that ₹2 lakh sat in the loan for only about four years, and I paid roughly **₹60,000** in additional interest before I closed it out. That brought the real cost of the "₹2 lakh" premium to about **₹2.60 lakh.**

But the more honest comparison – and the one I want to walk through carefully – is *what would have happened if I'd done what most home-loan borrowers actually do, and let the loan and the bundled insurance run for the full 20 years.*

The Full Math: Bundled Insurance vs Pure Term Till 60

Let's set up two parallel scenarios. Same person (me, 32, healthy, 2018). Same goal (₹2 crore of life cover for my family). Two structures.

Scenario A - Bundled credit life, run for the full 20 years.

- One-time premium: ₹2,00,000, financed inside the home loan at 8.5%.
- Effective EMI bump from this slice: roughly ₹1,735 a month.
- Over 240 months, total cash paid on the premium slice: about ₹4.16 lakh - that is **₹2 lakh of premium plus ₹2.16 lakh of interest.**
- The cover starts at ₹2 crore and decreases as the loan principal decreases. At year 1 the cover is ~₹2 cr; by year 10 it's roughly ₹1.3 cr; by year 20 it is essentially zero.
- Average cover over those 20 years: roughly ₹1 crore.
- Cover for years 21 through to my 60th birthday (8 years): zero. The loan, and therefore the policy, has ended.

Scenario B - A pure online term plan, taken till age 60.

- Annual premium for a ₹2 crore cover, 32-year-old in 2018: roughly ₹18,000 a year (the going market rate then).
- Term: 28 years, till age 60.
- Total nominal cash out over 28 years: about ₹5.04 lakh.
- Cover stays flat at ₹2 crore for the entire 28 years. Doesn't shrink. Doesn't depend on the loan. Doesn't disappear if I prepay or refinance.
- If I die at 45 with the loan two-thirds paid, my family still gets ₹2 crore.
- If I die at 58 with the house long since paid off, my family still gets ₹2 crore.

Now compare the two side by side.

	Bundled credit life (20 yr)	**Pure term till 60 (28 yr)**
Total cash out	~₹4.16 lakh	~₹5.04 lakh
Cover at start	₹2 crore	₹2 crore
Cover at end	₹0	₹2 crore
Average cover	~₹1 crore	₹2 crore
Years of protection	20	28

For roughly **20% more nominal money,** the pure term plan gives me **flat ₹2 crore cover for 8 more years** and **twice the average cover** during the overlapping 20-year period.

The sharper way to look at it is "cost per crore per year of protection delivered":

- **Bundled:** ₹4.16 lakh paid, ~20 crore-years of cover (₹1 cr average × 20 yr). That's about **₹20,800 per crore per year.**
- **Pure term:** ₹5.04 lakh paid, 56 crore-years of cover (₹2 cr × 28 yr). That's about **₹9,000 per crore per year.**

For every rupee of *actual protection* I bought, the bundled product cost me **more than 2x** what a clean term plan would have cost. And it left me uncovered for the most financially complicated years of my life - the ones between the home loan ending and retirement starting, which happen to be precisely the years a family most needs the safety net.

I had paid more, gotten less, locked into a structure that died with the loan, and funded a six-figure NBFC commission along the way. To save 0.1% of the processing fee.

The 0.1% processing fee waiver was, in pure rupee terms, the most expensive discount I have ever taken.

The Bigger Picture

This chapter is not really about insurance. It's about the bundling trick – the move where a bank or NBFC sells you a financial product as part of another financial product, in a moment when you are too distracted, too tired, or too eager to close the deal to think clearly about it.

It happens with home loans (credit life, "loan protection insurance"). It happens with car loans (auto insurance bundled with the EMI). It happens at the car dealership (the dealer-pushed insurance package that's pricier than the same policy bought online). It happens with credit cards (personal accident cover, "free for the first year"). It happens at airports (the forex card upgrade with travel insurance).

The pattern is always the same: the second product is priced badly, sold opaquely, locked into the first product, and exists primarily because the bank earns a fat distributor commission on it. The waiver/discount/freebie that makes you say yes is almost always smaller than the cost of the bundled product.

What did I learn?

First: *never buy insurance from the entity giving you the loan.* They are conflicted. They make money on the spread, and on the commission. The product is, by definition, not optimised for you. It is optimised for the loan officer's quarterly target. Buy your insurance separately, online, from a different company, after comparing rates.

Second: *always ask "what is this costing me, fully loaded?"* Not just the headline price. Add interest if it's financed. Subtract the discount they offered to make you say yes. Compute the net. Most bundled products lose this comparison badly.

Third: *decreasing cover is not real cover.* Credit life pays your bank back. Pure term pays your family. They are not substitutes. If you only have credit life and no pure term, your family is protected only as long as the bank is. After that, they are on their own.

Fourth, the meta-lesson: t*he moments when you are most likely to say yes to a bad financial product are the moments when you are signing for a big one.* Buying a house. Taking a car loan. Getting a credit card. Closing a mortgage refinance. In every one of these moments, somebody will hand you a brochure and say "while we're at it..." Train yourself, in those moments, to slow down. Take the brochure. Say, "Let me think about it." Walk out. Decide tomorrow, when you are not in transaction mode.

The bank knows you are tired. That's exactly why they pull the brochure out then.

I paid ~₹60,000 in interest, and an unknowable amount in commissions, to learn this. You can have the lesson for the price of this book.

Mistake #7, logged. Eight more to go.

CHAPTER

08

Nysha Was Born. I Started Investing for Her Three Years Late

October 2019. My daughter Nysha was born. I will not try to describe how that felt, because every parent who has been in that delivery-room moment has the same feeling and no language for it, and every non-parent will find any attempt at description, slightly nauseating.

So let me skip the feelings and go to the spreadsheet, which is what this book is about.

By November, my dad-brain had locked onto a list. It was the most Indian-uncle list ever conceived:

- Aadhaar. ✓
- Passport. ✓

- PAN. ✓
- Bank account in her name. ✓
- Investment plan for her future. ← this is where the wheels came off.

I wanted to start investing for her on Day 1. Not because I'd read some book about compounding and time horizons, but because every parent in India is haunted by the same number – *the cost of a 2040 college education.* You hear it from relatives. You hear it from financial advisors at weddings. You hear it from the LIC agent who somehow has your number. *College fees doubling every seven years. Kids going abroad. Coaching classes. Sports. Marriage.* The Indian parent's compound-anxiety machine.

So I did what any sleep-deprived new dad in finance does. I went deep into research mode.

And here is what I learned, after six weeks of reading: 99% of "child plans" sold in India are *garbage.*

Not 50%. Not 80%. Ninety-nine percent.

I will not name names, because legal constraints, but if you have ever been pitched a "Children's Future Plan" with a teddy bear on the brochure – that thing is a ULIP (Unit Linked Insurance Plan) wearing a costume. The "Smart Child" insurance plan? Endowment policy with a smaller surrender penalty. The mutual fund with "child" in its name? Almost all are funds with a five-year lock-in stapled to it and a slightly higher expense ratio for the privilege of having "child" in the name. The lock-in does not protect your child. It protects the AMC's (Asset Management Company's) and Insurance Companies AUM (Assets Under Management).

The fundamental, frustrating truth I came to was this: *a child has no separate need for a separate financial product.* A child needs a goal-aligned portfolio: a mix of equity, gold and debt, with a horizon long enough to ride out cycles, and discipline. That's it. The child doesn't care if the fund has a teddy bear on it. Compounding is, mercifully, indifferent to the marketing.

What I did, in the end, was put ₹1.5 lakh per year into Sukanya Samriddhi Yojana – the government's scheme for the girl child, which gives a fixed, tax-free, sovereign-backed return that is simple, boring, and impossible to mess up. I felt good about myself. I told my wife, "We're sorted." I patted myself on the back. I went to sleep.

This is the part where the actual mistake begins, and it is sneakier than anything I've talked about so far.

Because here is what I *thought* I was doing: investing for my daughter.

And here is what I was actually doing: making one disciplined annual contribution to one government scheme, while the other 95% of our family's wealth – equity, MFs, the home, savings – was sitting in my name, unallocated, in one undifferentiated pool I mentally called "ours."

Nothing was earmarked for her. Nothing was tagged to her timelines. There was no separate compounding clock running for her goals.

For three years, I told myself I was investing for Nysha because I was paying into Sukanya. In reality, I was running the entire family's portfolio as if she didn't exist as a financial entity, and patting myself on the back for one small, government-mandated SIP.

The cost of this was not obvious at first. Sukanya was doing fine. Markets were doing fine. On the surface, the portfolio looked healthy.

The problem was *asset allocation*.

When I sat down to plan our money, my horizons in my head were my horizons: retirement at 60, a vague goal somewhere at 5–7 years out, etc. Those horizons drove my equity-debt mix. I was running a *medium-duration* portfolio for a household that, in reality, had a bunch of *very long-duration* obligations sitting inside it that I had never named.

If I had carved out, on Day 1 of Nysha being born, a specific bucket – say, "Nysha 2039 college" – and run that bucket as a 20-year, equity-heavy portfolio, the math is not subtle. Two decades, mostly equity, in Indian markets is the kind of horizon that turns small monthly amounts into sentence-finishing numbers.

Instead, I started doing it properly only when she was about three years old. I lost three years of compounding on a bucket that needed every year it could get.

When my son was born in 2024, I was determined not to repeat the lesson. So I went the next step – I created a Hindu Undivided Family (HUF) structure, started routing investments specifically tagged to both kids through it, and gave each child their own clean, named, time-horizon-matched allocation.

(Worth a separate note: an HUF is a useful structure for some families because it has its own PAN and gets its own basic exemption – but it has its own complexities, and you should talk to a CA before setting one up. I will not give you tax advice in a book. I will only confess to my own mistakes.)

The HUF was the operational fix. The mental fix was bigger.

It was learning to stop thinking of household wealth as one monolithic blob that "belongs to me, the dad" and starting to think of it as a portfolio of named buckets, each with its own owner, horizon, and asset mix.

What did I learn?

First: *time, not product, is what makes a child portfolio work*. A boring index fund started on Day 1 will eat almost any clever child-themed product started at Year 5. There is no fancy instrument. There is just early, consistent, equity-heavy compounding, and the only way to access it is to start when the child is young enough to not have an opinion about ice cream.

Second: *if it's not named, it's not allocated.* Money that lives in your general portfolio "for the family" is not earmarked for any goal. It's earmarked for whatever crisis or temptation comes up first. The act of opening a separate folio, naming it "Nysha – College – 2039," and watching it grow over years is what stops you from accidentally tapping it for something else.

Third: *every "child plan" with a teddy bear, a tagline, or a celebrity is, until proven otherwise, an insurance product in costume.* Mix of regular term insurance for protection + plain-vanilla equity SIPs for growth + a small, boring sovereign instrument like Sukanya/PPF for stability does the job of every child plan ever sold, at a fraction of the cost.

Fourth, and this is the lesson I wish someone had handed me in the maternity ward: *the moment your child is born, you have just acquired a new, very long-duration financial liability with a name and a face.* Treat it like that. Open a folio. Name it. Tag it. Start it. The hospital paperwork takes a week. The financial paperwork takes an afternoon. Do not let "I'll set it up properly later" turn into "Nysha is five and I haven't started."

Future Nysha is going to read this someday. Probably at 20, probably while rolling her eyes. To her, in advance: I'm sorry I lost you three years of compounding because I confused "I love you" with "I am financially ready for you." I'm doing better now. Your brother got the upgraded version of dad.

Mistake #8, logged. Seven more to go.

CHAPTER

09

The ULIP I Bought for My Niece (and Other Bad Gifts)

I have, over the years, given my niece Ananya many gifts. A toy kitchen. A weirdly elaborate dollhouse. A bicycle that she has, last I checked, mildly outgrown. A few books she pretended to read because I was watching.

The single worst gift I have ever given her was, on paper, the most thoughtful one.

Ananya was born in June 2011 – eight years before my own daughter Nysha. As her uncle, I have always wanted to give her something that mattered when she actually became old enough to need it. Not toys. Not clothes. Money. Real, compounded, when-you're-twenty-and-thinking-about-college-or-a-business kind of money.

So somewhere around 2020, when she was nine, I decided I was going to do this *properly*. I wasn't going to just stick a fixed deposit in her name and forget about it. I was going to *research*. I was a banker. I knew how to read a fact sheet. I was going to find the right product.

What followed is one of the more humbling things I have to admit in this book: a man who spent thirteen years analysing capital structures, who could read a prospectus in his sleep, walked into a popular online insurance marketplace, did several days of "research," and bought a ULIP.

For a child.

Through a website.

I'd like to take a moment, on behalf of past-Harsh, to apologise to present-Ananya. I can only hope future-Ananya never reads this chapter, or if she does, that she's earning enough by then to find it funny.

A Quick Refresher on Why ULIPs Are Bad (Especially for Children)

For readers who haven't been mis-sold one yet – congratulations, please skip to the next paragraph and never look back – a ULIP, or Unit Linked Insurance Plan, is a hybrid product that combines life insurance with investment in market-linked funds. The pitch sounds elegant: *"Your money grows in the markets, AND you get a life cover, AND there are tax benefits, AND it builds a corpus for your child's future. All in one product."*

It is, in practice, almost always one of the worst products you can buy in Indian retail finance. Here is why.

The fees. ULIPs have layers and layers of charges. A premium allocation charge – money taken off the top before it even gets invested. A policy administration charge – monthly. A mortality charge – for the insurance bit. A fund management charge – for the investment bit. A switching charge if you move between funds. A surrender charge if you exit early. By the time the actual market money is doing its actual market thing, somewhere between 5% and 15% of your premium in the early years has gone to fees. Compare that to a direct mutual fund, where the all-in expense ratio is often 0.5%–1.5% per year. Different sport.

The lock-in. ULIPs lock your money for a minimum of 5 years. If you exit early, the surrender charges are punitive. So even if you realise within a year that you've made a mistake, you can't cleanly get out without giving up a meaningful chunk.

The "insurance" is bad insurance. The life cover inside a ULIP is typically modest – often 10x the annual premium, which on a ₹50,000-a-year plan is ₹5 lakh. For an actual term plan that gives you, say, ₹1 crore of cover, you'd pay ₹10,000–15,000 a year separately. The ULIP makes you pay for both the bad insurance and the bad investment, in one expensive package.

The "investment" is bad investment. Returns on most ULIP funds I have tracked over 5-7 years have lagged plain-vanilla equity mutual funds, sometimes by several percentage points a year. The drag from fees compounds the wrong way.

For a child, it's worse. Children don't need life insurance – there is no income to insure. They need a long-horizon, low-cost, equity-heavy compounding machine. Wrapping that in a 5%-fee insurance product just to put the word "child" in the brochure is an act of marketing, not finance.

My Particular Mistake

I bought the ULIP in 2020. I picked one of the bigger brand-name companies. I picked it through one of the larger online insurance platforms, which I had, somewhere in my head, equated with "transparent pricing" – as if the platform was on my side. (The platform earns a commission. The platform was not on my side. The platform was a beautifully designed display case.)

I started paying the premium. ULIP statements arrive once a year, attractively designed to obscure exactly the metric you should be tracking. I would glance at the "fund value" once a year and think, *"Hmm, that looks like it's growing."* I did not benchmark it against anything. That was, of course, the whole design.

Five or six years in, in early 2025, I sat down to actually compare.

The ULIP fund value was, after all premiums and fees, worse than what the same money would have done in a basic FD over the same period. Not "slightly worse than equity." *Worse than a fixed deposit.* The fees, plus a couple of unfortunate fund choices inside the ULIP, plus general drag, had eaten so much of the return that even sovereign debt would have done better.

If I had simply opened a low-cost equity index fund SIP in Ananya's name with the same monthly amount, the corpus today would have been somewhere between 1.5x and 1.7x what the ULIP shows. For her at twenty, the difference between those two outcomes is probably the difference between "nice gift from uncle" and "actually-meaningful starting capital for whatever she wants to do."

I had, with all the best intentions and all the worst execution, given her the most expensive piece of paper I have ever signed. I have since switched her into a far better-structured plan - late, but at least done.

What I'd Do Today (And What I Now Tell Friends With Newborn Nieces and Nephews)

If you want to give a child in your family a financial gift that actually matters by the time they grow up, here is the menu, in rough order of how badly each one underperforms the top of the list:

Best: A monthly SIP in a low-cost, broad-based equity fund – a Nifty 50 index fund, a flexi-cap fund, or a combination – in the child's name (or held in your name and earmarked for them, with a clear note in your will). Eighteen to twenty years of compounding in equities, even at modest amounts, is the kind of math that produces sentence-finishing numbers. Charges: ~0.5%-1% a year, all-in. SEBI is soon going to introduce the gifting of mutual funds via prepaid cards.

Good: Sukanya Samriddhi Yojana for a girl child, or PPF, or a sovereign tax-free instrument. Lower returns than equity, but rock-solid, sovereign-backed, no fee drag. A great base layer alongside the SIP above. Don't make this the whole gift, but it's a fine part of it.

Acceptable: A simple bank FD, opened and rolled over. Boring, low-return, but transparent. You at least know what you're getting.

Better than nothing: A regular mutual fund (slightly higher expense ratio than direct, because of distributor commission). Still beats the ULIP.

Avoid: *Anything* with the word "child" in the brand name and a smiling kid on the brochure. Not because all of them are scams

– some are perfectly legal products – but because the marketing-to-substance ratio is consistently terrible. Whatever you'd buy a child, you can buy in a generic version that does the same job better and cheaper.

Avoid harder: ULIPs, endowment plans, "money-back" policies, "child plans," and anything sold as a "complete solution." These are products designed to look like they cover everything because the seller earns a higher commission on a bundled product. Insurance + investment + child + tax saving in one product means *bad insurance + bad investment + bad child planning + meh tax saving,* in one fee structure. *(This is my personal view, not investment advice - talk to a fee-only planner for your situation.)*

What did I learn?

First: *the platform is not your friend.* Online insurance marketplaces, online stockbrokers, online "financial supermarkets" – they all have a business model. That model is, almost universally, distributor commissions on the products they push to the top of the list. The platform is a salesperson with better UI (User Interface), not an advisor.

Second: *separate insurance from investment, always.* Buy your insurance through a pure term plan from a transparent insurer. Buy your investment through a pure mutual fund or stock. Anything that tries to do both, in one product, is either incompetently designed or designed to confuse you. Usually the latter.

Third: *for a child, time horizon is the only real edge.* The single biggest determinant of how much money your gift becomes by the time the kid is twenty is the *number of years the money compounded* and the *expense ratio drag.* A 0.5%-fee equity index fund started on day 1 will eat almost any clever child-themed product started at year 5. Time and low fees beat product design, every time.

Fourth, the meta-lesson: *research is not the same as analysis.* I did "research" on the ULIP for a week. I read brochures. I compared three companies. I picked the "best" one. What I did not do was *zoom out and ask whether the entire category was the right one.* I had been comparing apples within a basket of bad apples, and proudly picked the one with the least visible bruise.

The next time you find yourself comparing three options for a financial decision, ask yourself the harder question: *is this the right basket of options, or am I about to pick the best of a bad set?* That's the question past-Harsh did not ask, and Ananya's ULIP statement is the price of him not asking it.

I have since been very deliberate about not buying anything similar – for myself, for my own children, or for anyone else's. The ULIP for Ananya has now been replaced with a better-structured plan; I fixed the mistake, just too late for the early-compounding years to come back. The rest of her growing-up corpus is being built – properly, this time – through a clean, named, equity-heavy SIP that I should have started in 2020 in the first place.

Mistake #9, logged. Six more to go.

CHAPTER

10

The Conversation I Should Have Had With My Parents Ten Years Earlier

This is the chapter I have been avoiding writing.

I have written the funny chapters and the embarrassing chapters. I have happily made jokes at my own expense about credit cards and crypto and an Andheri secretary. This one isn't funny. It's the one where I tell you about the most expensive financial mistake of my life – measured not just in rupees, but in the months and years I spent untangling something I should have known about long before I had to.

Let me set the scene.

I moved to Mumbai for my MBA in 2007. I built my career there. I got married to Nilisha in 2013. By the late 2010s, I was, by every external measure, doing well. A demanding job at a top investment bank. A life in the city.

My parents lived in Bhopal. My father ran a medicine business he had built for two decades. A family business in the truest sense – the kind that quietly puts kids through college and runs a household with dignity. He was good at what he did. He was proud of it. I was proud of him.

And here is the thing I am still – nine years later – embarrassed to say out loud:

I had absolutely no idea how the financial side of his life worked.

Not in a "broad strokes I don't know the details" way. In a "I genuinely could not have answered any of the basic questions" way. I did not know what bank accounts he had. I did not know who his CA was. I did not know what insurance he had, or didn't have. I did not know which customers or dealers owed him money, and which suppliers he owed money to. I did not know where his important documents were physically stored.

I knew he was doing fine. I knew he was happy. I knew he loved his grandchildren. And I assumed that because I was busy building my career, the kindest thing I could do was *not bother him with my questions*. I was wrong about that. I was wrong about that in a way I cannot fully describe.

In 2017, my father passed away. Suddenly.

There is no graceful way to write that sentence and there is no graceful way to live through it. I will not pretend to.

What followed, on top of the grief, was a financial situation I was wholly unprepared for.

The Aftermath Nobody Prepares You For

When you run a family-owned business in India for decades, your books look something like this: piles of paper bills, a notebook with handwritten entries, money you've given to people on trust, money people owe you on trust, suppliers, distributors, retailers, friends-who-borrowed-and-said-they'd-pay-soon, and an entire web of informal credit that exists only in your head and in the heads of the people you do business with.

That web does not survive the person who built it.

When my father passed, I had to wind everything down. I had to close the business. I had to settle the assets. I had to figure out who owed what to whom and reconcile a ledger that had no neat double-entry book to refer to.

Here is what happened, in the most predictable, painful pattern you can imagine.

The people who were owed money by my father came forward. Promptly. With their bills, their notes, their voices raised, their stories of how he had promised to pay them by Diwali, Holi, the next quarter. Some of these claims were real. Some, almost certainly, were not. I had no way of telling the two apart, because the only person who had known the difference was no longer here. So I paid. I paid out of my own pocket, from the savings I had built up over eight years of investment banking. I paid because the alternative was an indignity to my father's name that I was not willing to entertain. I paid more than I should have, knowing some of it was probably inflated, because grief and pride are a very expensive combination at a settlement table.

The people who owed money to my father did not come forward. Not promptly. Not later. Not at all. Some of them, I knew about because my father had once mentioned a name. Most of them, I didn't. Without his ledger in my head, there was no way to chase, prove, or recover. The money owed to him quietly evaporated into the same notebooks where it had always lived.

By 2018-19, I had drained almost the entire eight years of savings I had carefully built up.

Now – and I want to say this clearly, because I do not want this chapter to read as a complaint – I do not regret a single rupee of what I paid. He was my father. The settling of his affairs was my responsibility. I would do every single one of those payments again.

What I do regret, deeply and permanently, is the thing that made all of it harder than it had to be: *I had never sat down with him, in his lifetime, and had the simple conversation.*

The Conversation That Would Have Changed Everything

Imagine if, somewhere around 2012 or 2013 – when life was calm and there was no urgency – I had said to him:

"Papa, can we sit down sometime this Diwali, just for an hour? Tell me where your accounts are. Show me the notebook. Tell me who owes you, who you owe. Let me know who your CA is. Show me where the documents are. Not so I can run anything. Just so I know."

That conversation – one hour, every couple of years – would have spared us both years of pain after he was gone.

I would have known which claims to question and which to honour. I would have had names. I would have known which bills were active and which were dormant. I would have had his ledger, in some form, in my own head.

It is a peculiar Indian tragedy that most of us go our entire lives never having this conversation with our parents. We treat their finances as their private domain, which is partly out of respect and partly out of cultural awkwardness. We think asking is intrusive. We think it implies we are waiting for them to die, or planning for it, or – worse – angling for something. So we don't ask. And then, one day, we have to.

The right time to have that conversation is not when something has gone wrong. The right time is exactly when nothing is wrong. When the conversation can be light. When it can happen over tea, with no pressure. When the answer to "what would happen if..." is hypothetical, not imminent.

What I Tell Friends Now

When friends – especially friends in their thirties, with parents in their sixties – tell me they're "thinking they should probably get organised," I tell them three things.

First, *just have the conversation.* Once. This year. Not a financial audit. Not an interrogation. A conversation. *"I want to know enough that, if anything happens, I'm not lost. Will you help me?"* Most parents, in my experience, are quietly relieved. Many of them have been wanting to share this and didn't know how to bring it up.

Second, *make a single, simple list together.* Not in a fancy planner. A piece of paper, or a Google Doc, or a note on the phone.

Bank accounts. Investments. Insurance policies. Loans (theirs and owed to them). Property documents. CA's name. Lawyer's name (if any). Where the physical documents are stored. Nominees and beneficiaries on each. That's it. One page. Update it once a year.

Third, *digitise as much as you can, while everyone's around to confirm.* Today, in 2026, the tools exist. There are apps and platforms – including, I will quietly mention, the one we are building at NYVO – designed exactly to help families consolidate this kind of information in one place. Even if you don't use any app, even if you do it on a Google Drive folder shared between you and a sibling, the act of putting it somewhere accessible changes everything.

One more, painful, learning from my own experience: *surrender your parents' PAN cards and close their tax records once they are gone.* I did not and. Two years after my father had passed, an income-tax notice arrived in his name, demanding ₹26 lakh in tax dues. I had no documents, no books, no way to mount a clean defence. After months of running around, the matter was finally settled at ₹13 lakh under the income tax scheme of Vivad se Vishwas - a number I paid out of pocket, on top of everything else, simply because nobody had taught me that the to-do list after a parent's death includes their tax file too.

There is no neat numbered list at the end of this chapter, and there is not going to be one. I would give back every rupee I made in investment banking to have had one more Diwali with my father, sitting on the sofa, going through his notebook with him, asking him to explain it all to me. The conversation costs nothing. The avoidance of the conversation costs everything. If you are reading this and your parents are still around, please – pick up the phone today. Let the conversation not be about money. But just to say hi. And then, somewhere in the next three months, find a quiet evening, and have the conversation. The fact that you can still have it is a privilege. Most of us only realise that when it is no longer one.

Mistake #10, logged. Five more to go.

CHAPTER

11

The Day I Killed My Home Loan – and ₹1.5 Crore of Compounding

In 2018, I booked a house. The very next thought I had – before the keys, before the curtains, before figuring out what a "society maintenance charge" was – was: *how do I pay this off as fast as humanly possible?*

This is, I have come to learn, an extremely Indian thought.

For thirteen years I had been doing 16-hour days in investment banking. Kotak. Bank of America. IPO after IPO, deal after deal. Somewhere in there I had built up the only definition of freedom my brain seemed to recognise – zero EMIs. No credit card balance. No car loan. No home loan. The Indian middle-class dream, in financial-product form. Pay everything off, sleep peacefully, die debt-free.

So when I joined Bank of America, I worked like a man on a deadline. I was. The deadline was just one I hadn't told anyone about: the home loan.

Then came February 2022.

In foreign banks, the bonus cycle runs January to December, and the cheque lands in February. 2021 had been a post-COVID boom year. The bonus was – let's just say – *very satisfying.* On 25th February I got the credit. On 28th February I walked into HDFC Ltd, prepaid ₹1.5 crore of outstanding home loan in a single shot, and walked out feeling like I had ascended to a higher plane of consciousness.

I came back to office and resigned an hour later.

That afternoon, sitting at my desk with no home loan, no car loan, no credit card balance, no manager, and a pretty good idea of where I was headed next, I genuinely thought: *I have done it. I am free.* I called my wife. I think I said something dramatic like, "Babe, no liability." She said something like, "Cool, let's go out for dinner."

In April that same year, we shifted to Bangalore. I joined a fintech startup. The salary was solid. Life was good. Mistake, mostly invisible, slowly began to do its work.

Here is what I had not understood.

The home loan I was so triumphantly killing was at roughly 7% (after rate cuts, it had come to 7% from original 8.5%) interest, of which a meaningful chunk was tax-deductible under Section 24(b) and (then) 80C. Effective post-tax cost of that loan, for someone in the highest tax bracket, was somewhere closer to 5%.

Possibly less.

Now, here are the actual numbers, because this book is allergic to vibes-based math.

On 28 February 2022 – the day I walked out of HDFC feeling like a samurai – the Nifty 50 closed at **16,793**. The day I am writing this, in early May 2026, it is sitting around **24,000**. That works out to a **43% absolute return** over roughly four-and-a-bit years. As a CAGR (Compound Annual Growth Rate) – the way fund managers and gym trainers prefer to flex their numbers – that's about **9% a year**.

That is not a moonshot. The Nifty did not double. I had told myself, in a few comforting moments since 2022, that "it would have doubled at least, no?" – the way every Indian who has missed an investment slightly inflates the parallel-universe number to manage their guilt. The actual number, when you make yourself look at it, is more humbling and more useful: a slow, steady, mostly-boring 9% a year. With one strong run-up to ~26,000 in late 2024 and a 2025-26 correction stapled on the end, just to keep things interesting.

But – and this is the part I had to sit with – *9% is still meaningfully more than the post-tax cost of the loan I killed*. And nobody who'd worked in finance for thirteen years was going to put ₹1.5 crore in a pure index fund anyway. That's not how I would have invested. So let me stop being kind to my past self and run the actually-realistic counterfactual.

The honest counterfactual is a 50/50 split – half in a Nifty 50 index fund, half in a flexi-cap fund. That is exactly what an informed Indian investor with my profile would have done. Index for the boring base. Flexi-cap (Parag Parikh, HDFC Flexi Cap, ICICI Pru Flexi – the usual suspects) for the active layer that flexes across large-, mid-, and small-cap depending on where the manager sees value.

Here is what those two halves did, between Feb 2022 and May 2026:

- **Nifty 50** – ~9% CAGR. ₹75 lakh → ~₹1.07 crore.
- **Flexi-cap (mainstream brand-name funds)** – Parag Parikh Flexi Cap delivered ~17% CAGR. HDFC Flexi Cap, ~18%. The category average over this 4-year window sits around 15%. Take the middle: 15-17% CAGR. ₹75 lakh → roughly **₹1.34 to 1.44 crore**.
- **Combined** – somewhere in the **₹2.40 to 2.50 crore** range, today.

(A fair caveat on this math: the actual counterfactual should also net off the interest I'd have paid on the running home loan over those four years - and add back the ~₹50,000 a month in rent the flat was generating. Both adjustments narrow the gap a bit, but the direction of the answer doesn't change.)

Now subtract the ₹1.5 crore I started with. The 50/50 portfolio I did not have would have grown to nearly **double** my prepayment, in a window that included a brutal 2025-26 correction. Net gain: somewhere between ₹*90 lakh and* ₹*1 crore.*

Compare that to what I actually got from killing the loan: a saving equivalent to compounding ₹1.5 crore at ~5% post-tax over the same period – roughly **₹1.83 crore in equivalent terms**, or a notional gain of ₹33 lakh.

So the real opportunity cost – the one I'd been too lazy and too guilty to actually compute – is closer to **₹55 to 65 lakh**, not ₹30 lakh.

That's not a Maruti every year. That's a second small flat. That's Nysha's college, fully funded, in advance. That's roughly two years of a startup founder's salary.

That's the price tag on my "no liability" feeling. And I had never written it down.

Worse – that prepayment was sunk into a property that, over those same four years, gave me effectively zero capital appreciation. The rental yield was fine. The capital growth was a heart-rate monitor on a man taking a long nap. So I'd taken liquid, productive capital out of an asset class that was about to compound beautifully and used it to extinguish a cheap, tax-advantaged loan that was sitting on top of an asset that was, frankly, doing nothing.

I had paid 100 paise to remove a debt that was costing me 50 paise – and given up 130 paise of return in the process.

This was, in pure rupee terms, the single most expensive decision of my career.

Now, here is where I have to be honest, because honesty is the entire point of this book.

Even today, sitting with the math, knowing exactly what it cost me – *I do not fully regret it.*

At 35, I became, in the most boring middle-class sense of the word, free. No EMI alerts. No bank reminders. No call from any relationship manager asking me to "consider a top-up." If the startup didn't work out, my house was mine. If the next bonus didn't come, my house was mine. If life decided to mess with me, my house was mine.

There is a kind of psychological capital in that, and I won't pretend it has no value. For a guy who'd just walked out of a 13-year career and was about to bet on himself, having nothing on the liability side of the balance sheet was, in some way, what gave me the nerve to do it.

But that's a feeling. And feelings, as I am slowly learning, are very expensive when you let them run your spreadsheet.

The one-line rule I now live by: *cheap, tax-advantaged debt is leverage, not a curse. Kill the expensive stuff first; let the cheap stuff run.*

Everything in this chapter – the ₹60 lakh of opportunity cost, the four years of compounding I traded away, the misplaced "no liability" feeling – flows from forgetting that one sentence. We Indians are emotionally trained to treat every loan as something to be slain, and most of the time, killing the cheapest loan on the balance sheet is exactly the wrong move.

If, on 28th February 2022, I had been forced to articulate in one paragraph to my future self – *"I am paying off this home loan because..."* – I would not have been able to finish the sentence without admitting the real reason was emotional, not financial. The peace of mind was real. The cost of that peace of mind was extremely real, too. The most expensive financial decisions of your life rarely feel like financial decisions at all. They feel like clarity. They feel like *ghar ka loan khatam karna hai.* Run the parallel-universe spreadsheet anyway. Always.

Mistake #11, logged. Four more to go.

CHAPTER

12

The Stock Strategies That Never Made Me Money

For the better part of thirteen years, I was not really allowed to trade stocks.

I mean that almost literally. From sometime around 2015 onwards, the compliance rules at investment banks tightened to the point of comedy. At Kotak, you needed pre-clearance for almost any trade and a six-month minimum holding period. By the time I got to Bank of America, I couldn't even hold most stocks unless they were grandfathered in from before I joined. Mutual funds and government bonds – fine. Direct equity – basically off-limits.

This was, I now realise, the best thing that could have happened to my net worth.

Because the day I left Bank of America in February 2022, I opened a fresh demat account, looked at the screen, and thought: *now I am going to play.*

What followed was, in hindsight, one of the more expensive personal finance trips I have ever taken – disguised as a learning curve.

Phase 1: Buying Everything (the "kid in a candy store" era)

For the first year out, I tried *everything*.

I bought direct stocks. I bought baskets – every baskets via platform you've heard of, and a couple you haven't. I bought sectoral baskets. I bought consumer baskets. I bought thematic baskets. I bought "AI revolution" and "EV revolution" and "the next decade of India" and a basket whose theme I genuinely cannot reconstruct anymore.

I tried F&O (Futures & Options). Not seriously, not with full size – but enough to learn that knowing how options are priced and *making money on them* are two completely different sports.

I dabbled in algo trading. I read about momentum strategies. I built a small spreadsheet that I checked compulsively. I owned, at one point, something like 30+ individual stocks across half a dozen "themes," and I could not have told you with a straight face why I owned any single one of them at the size I owned it.

The result was exactly what every retail investor figures out the long way: I was *spreading myself so thin that even when I picked something right, the position size was too small to matter, and even when I picked something wrong, there were enough other positions to mask it for months.* I wasn't building a portfolio. I was building a participation trophy.

I lost a decent amount of money. I will not give you the exact number because the exact number is between me, my CA.

Phase 2: PMS (the "let's pay someone smarter" era)

Eventually, I did what every chastened retail investor in India does after a year of losses: I told myself the problem was that I shouldn't be picking stocks myself, and the solution was to hand the money to a *Portfolio Management Service*. Pay them a 2% management fee plus a performance share. Let the professionals do it.

PMS was, on paper, the grown-up move.

The actual results were – and I am being kind here – *fine*.

Not bad. Not great. *Fine*. Across the period I was in the PMS, my returns were worse than what I would have got from a basic flexi-cap mutual fund. The PMS had higher fees, similar volatility, and slightly worse performance.

The fund managers were smart. The framework was clean. The reports were beautifully formatted. The alpha was, for me, somewhere between absent and imaginary.

This is the part of the story where I have to be careful, because many PMSes do generate real alpha for the right kind of investor with the right time horizon. I am not saying PMS is a bad product. I am saying it was a bad product *for me, at that point, with what I was paying*. And one detail worth flagging for anyone considering one: PMS portfolios churn far more than mutual funds, which means short-term capital gains taxes can quietly eat another large chunk of your returns before the manager's alpha even shows up on a statement.

Phase 3: Sitting Down With a Clean Sheet of Paper

At some point in late 2023, I sat down– and forced myself to look at every single thing I had been doing.

What jumped out, when I lined it all up, was painfully simple:

I had been trying to capture every kind of alpha that existed.

Direct stocks for one alpha. F&O for another. Algo for a third. Sectoral baskets for fourth. PMS for fifth. Theme funds for sixth. I was running, simultaneously, half a dozen incompatible investment philosophies, each at half-strength, each undercutting the others, and each with its own fee.

I was not investing. I was *cosplaying* as six different kinds of investor at once.

So I deleted ninety percent of it.

For the last roughly two years, my approach has collapsed into something almost embarrassingly simple. It looks like this:

1. **Pick a stock based on fundamental analysis.** What does this company do? Is the business model sound? Are the unit economics improving? Is management capable and incentive-aligned? Is the price reasonable for the cashflow I expect over the next five to ten years? If I can't answer those questions in one paragraph, I don't buy.

2. **Decide the total amount I want to deploy in this stock.** Treat it as a real position, not a sprinkle.

3. **Deploy 50% on day one.** Get the position on the books.

4. **If the stock goes up, buy 25% more.** Add to winners.

5. **If the stock keeps going up, hold the remaining 25% in reserve. If it goes down, keep the other 25% for averaging.** Don't chase.

That's it. That's the whole "strategy." Five lines.

Two important footnotes before anyone copy-pastes this into their own demat account:

First, the 50-25-25 split is *mine*. It fits my temperament, my conviction levels, my willingness to add on the way up. Yours might be 30-30-40 or 100-on-day-one or something else entirely. The percentages are not the lesson. The discipline of *having a process* is.

Second, this is a strategy that works for me alongside a much larger boring core in low-cost index funds and a few flexi-caps. The direct-stock book is the active, conviction-led layer on top. It is not the whole portfolio. Nobody should run a hundred percent of their net worth this way.

What happened after I switched? Over the last roughly two years, I have made back everything I had lost in the F&O / Algo / PMS / basket carnival, and meaningfully more on top.

I didn't suddenly become a smarter investor. I got less clever, not more. I just stopped running six strategies at once and let one boring one breathe.

What I do today

The portfolio architecture I run today, after fifteen years of trial and error, fits on a Post-it:

1. **The boring core (75%).** Index funds, a couple of flexi-cap funds, gold and international investments. Set monthly. Reviewed quarterly. Touched almost never.

2. **The active layer (15-20%).** Five to seven direct stocks, each with a written one-paragraph thesis. Position-sized for conviction. The 50-25-25 deployment described above.

3. **Casino money (≤2%).** If I genuinely want to dabble in something I don't understand – a thematic basket, a single crypto, a friend's punt – it lives in this corner. I label it casino money out loud, so my future self can't pretend it was a strategy.

4. **No PMS. No F&O.** No daily trading. I have decided, in writing, that none of these are for me.

The single sentence that runs through all of it: *strategy proliferation is its own form of risk*. If you are running F&O, smallcases, stock baskets, direct stocks, PMS, and theme funds at the same time, you do not have a diversified portfolio. You have a confused one. Pick one philosophy, give it size, and let it breathe.

The strangest realisation, looking back, is that the trading restrictions at my old employers – no F&O, no penny stocks, hold periods on everything – were accidentally the best portfolio manager I ever had. They forced me into boring instruments for thirteen years. The years I was "free" to manage my own money were the years I lost the most. If you work somewhere with strict trading rules, stop seeing them as a cost. They are free behavioural insurance.

Mistake #12, logged. Three more to go.

CHAPTER

13

The Specialist I Never Hired

For thirteen years in investment banking, I was, in some narrow sense, a specialist.

Companies paid us – large, sophisticated companies with their own CFOs (Chief Financial Officers) and treasury teams and in-house finance shops – to come in and tell them how to raise capital, how to structure a debt facility, how to price an IPO or Bond offering. They had every reason to do this work themselves. They didn't, because they understood a simple thing that took me, embarrassingly, fifteen years of my own personal finance journey to internalise:

Even people who are very good at money are amateurs at their own money.

The CFOs who hired us were not stupid. They needed us to look at their own company from outside-in - partly for the regulatory reasons (an external banker has to sign off), but mostly for the simple fact that *your own balance sheet is the hardest one to read clearly.* They could have read the same prospectuses we read. They could have run the same comp sets. They hired us because doing your own work, on your own balance sheet, with your own emotions in the mix, is a structurally different sport from doing it for someone else. They were paying for *outside eyes.*

I never paid for outside eyes on my own portfolio. Not until very, very recently.

A Decade and a Half of "I've Got This"

For most of my career, my approach to my own money was a slightly more sophisticated version of the average urban Indian professional's approach: I read a lot, I followed a few people on the internet, I had opinions, I picked products, I opened a few apps, I rotated allocations when I felt like it, and I told myself that because I was *in finance,* I was probably doing this better than the average person.

The problem is, "better than the average person" is a really low bar in Indian personal finance.

Across roughly ten to sixteen years of investing on my own, here is what I had assembled, by sheer accumulation rather than by any plan:

- A few mutual funds, picked at different points in time for different reasons, none of which I had ever rationalised against each other
- Direct stocks bought across phases – some great, some terrible, some I had forgotten I owned

- A PMS, then no PMS, then ESOPs at three different employers
- Crypto that no longer existed
- A home loan I had aggressively paid off
- A couple of insurance policies, one good (the personal health policy), one bad (the loan-bundled term)
- A ULIP, in someone else's name, that I'd been pretending to ignore
- An EPF (Employee Provident Fund) account I had not looked at in years
- A bank account or three I no longer used

That is not a portfolio. That is the financial equivalent of an attic. Stuff has accumulated. None of it is throwing anything away. And there is no plan.

I had, technically, hired one specialist along the way: a CA, and that too only in the last six years. He has been excellent. The years before him were a quiet, slow, "I'll figure it out at filing time" disaster that cost me god-knows-how-much in suboptimal tax treatment.

But I had never, in fifteen years, paid a financial planner – somebody whose actual job is to look at the entire pile, ask questions I would rather not be asked, and tell me what to keep, what to rebalance, what to consolidate, and what to set on fire.

The Argument I Used to Have With Myself

Whenever the thought occurred to me – usually during some annual statement-reading exercise – I would have the same internal conversation, and I'd like to share it because I suspect every reader of this book has had a version of it.

"I work in finance. I read fact sheets for a living. Why would I pay someone else to do this?"

"Most of these planners are just selling commission products. I'd see right through them."

"I don't have that much money. A planner is for people with crore-plus portfolios."

"I'll just do it myself this weekend."

That last sentence is the most dangerous one. "I'll just do it myself this weekend" has an interesting property: the weekend never comes, but the sentence keeps you from hiring anyone else, because you have already promised yourself you will handle it. It is, functionally, a polite veto on getting outside help. Repeated four times a year, for fifteen years, that's sixty weekends I postponed exactly the same job.

What I was missing, in every one of those internal arguments, was the comparison I should have been running.

The question is not *"can I do this myself?"* I can. Of course I can.

The question is *"is the alpha I'd lose by doing it suboptimally – multiplied by all the weekends I postpone it – bigger than the fee a competent fee-only planner would charge me to do it properly?"*

For 99% of people, including me, the answer is yes. By a long way.

What Hiring a Specialist Actually Does

Let me describe, in concrete terms, what an outside set of eyes does that I could not do for myself, even though I knew the underlying mechanics perfectly well.

They make you write down your goals. Not in your head. On paper. *Retirement, kids' college, a down payment, an emergency fund, a lifestyle fund.* With amounts. With dates. The act of articulating these forces you to confront the fact that "saving for the future" is not a goal. It's a vibe.

They run an asset allocation against those goals. What percentage in equity, debt, gold, cash, real estate. *Why* in those percentages. They benchmark your current portfolio against this and show you the gap. Most professionals I know – myself emphatically included – discover that their actual portfolio looks nothing like what their goals would imply.

They consolidate your "attic." All those legacy accounts, dormant funds, half-forgotten policies, expired insurance, multiple EPF accounts from job changes. Either close them, transfer them, or actively own them. Stop having "stuff."

They force a regular review. Quarterly or annually. Not in your head. On a call. With minutes. *Did this happen? Did that happen? What's next?* This single discipline is, in my experience, worth more than any individual investment recommendation they will ever make.

They give you a second opinion at the moments you most need one. The crash of March 2020. A big bonus year. A job change. A health event. An inheritance. These are exactly the moments when your judgement is most likely to be compromised by emotion or context. Having somebody on the other end of an email saying *"don't sell," "yes invest the lump sum now," "no, don't move it all to that thing your cousin is excited about"* is, in pure rupee terms, often the difference between a great decade and a pedestrian one.

They are not paid by commissions. *A fee-only* planner earns a flat fee for their time and advice – not a cut of what you buy. This is critical. The Indian financial planning landscape has dramatically more *commission-paid* "advisors" than fee-only ones. The former are salespeople with a job title. The latter are the actual specialists.

What I Did About It

Honest answer: I have still not hired a fee-only planner.

What I have done, after fifteen-plus years of doing it badly, is sit down with a clean sheet of paper and finally put structure where there was none. The list of things that needed doing was not a secret - almost all of it was stuff I already knew:

- *Consolidate the mutual fund holdings into a leaner set.*
- *Tag every SIP to a goal. Name it. Date it.*
- *Increase equity weight in the long-horizon buckets; decrease it in the short-horizon ones.*
- *Close the dormant accounts.*
- *Treat the bad ULIP as dead money and stop adding to it.*
- *Calendar a six-monthly review, and actually do it.*

I worked my way down that list, slowly. I am, today, meaningfully better at this than I was at 30. The discipline of writing things down and reviewing them on a calendar - even alone - moved the needle far more than any single investment decision ever has.

But here is the harder thing I sit with: I had the time and the training do this on my own eventually. Most Indian families do not.

A good fee-only planner in India today charges ,₹25,000 to ,₹50,000 a year. For the family earning ,₹15-20 lakh a year that I have in mind when I think about who this book is for, that is a real number. It is the reason most of them never hire one, and end up with the kind of LIC-uncle-managed money piles.

This is the gap NYVO is built to close. We are building a personal financial planner for Indian families that costs a few hundred rupees a year - not thirty thousand. Flat fees. No commissions on any investment product, ever. Nobody on our side of the table makes a rupee more whether you buy any mutual fund, or nothing at all.

That structural cleanliness has been very hard to find in Indian retail finance. I know - I spent fifteen years looking for it, gave up, and ended up just figuring it out myself.

If I could go back and tell 30-year-old Harsh one thing about money – one single sentence – it would be this: *Pay somebody good, today, to look at your money with you, every quarter, for the rest of your life.*

That is, in many ways, the single thread that runs through every chapter of this book. It would have caught the credit card spiral early. It would have insisted on health insurance at 22, not 32. It would have stopped the ULIP for Ananya. It would have run the math before I prepaid the home loan. It would have killed the F&O experiments quickly. It would have built the emergency fund.

I'd rather you didn't take fifteen years to do what I should have done at twenty-five. The price of waiting is invisible. That is exactly why it bites.

Mistake #13, logged. Two more to go.

CHAPTER

14

The Upgrade Cycle (Phone, Watch, Car, Repeat)

In 2009, I started my first real job at ₹18,000 a month.

Net of rent, food, transport, and the occasional movie, my disposable income at that point was roughly the price of a decent dinner. Not a fancy dinner. A decent one. I budgeted for everything. I knew the price of every item on my regular grocery list. I felt every spend.

Across the next thirteen years, the salary went up. And up. And up. By the time I left Bank of America in 2022, my income – including bonuses – was something past-Harsh in 2009 would not have believed if you'd shown him the numbers in writing. Multiples and multiples of where it had started.

You might assume that the Harsh of 2022, with that kind of income, *felt* multiples richer than the Harsh of 2009.

He didn't.

He felt, on most days, *almost exactly the same.* Slightly better off. Less anxious about a bill here or there. But not richer in the qualitative, "I have so much more breathing room now", sense that you'd expect from a 20x or 30x rise in income.

That gap – between what should have happened and what actually did – is the entire chapter.

What Ate the Income

The standard explanation for this disappearing-income phenomenon is *lifestyle inflation.* The income rose; the expenses rose right along with it. True, but generic. Let me get specific, because the specifics are where the lesson lives.

Here's what actually happened, in roughly the order it happened.

The phone. In 2009 I had a Nokia. By 2012, an iPhone. By 2015, the latest iPhone. By 2018, the latest iPhone again, this time on EMI, "because the Pro Max is so much better." By 2022, I had upgraded the phone nine or ten times in thirteen years. Each upgrade felt like a small, justified treat. None of them, individually, was a big number. Cumulatively, somewhere in the realm of ₹6-8 lakh on phones I no longer own.

The watch. I held out for a long time on this one. Then, around 2016, the first proper "celebrate the bonus" watch. Then, every couple of years, an upgrade. Each one a step up. Each one with a story attached – *"this one I bought after we closed the X IPO," "this one was for my 35th birthday," "this one because I'd always wanted one."* Watches, unlike phones, don't depreciate to zero – but the upgrade habit is the same shape, just at a different price point. By the time I sat down to count, I owned thirty-two of them. I will let that sentence sit on the page without further comment.

The cars. This is the one I'm most embarrassed about, because I genuinely changed three cars in three years. Not because the previous one had broken. Not because my needs had changed. Because *the new one was better, and I could afford it, so why not?* I will spare you the brand names. The total damage, after depreciation and resale haircuts on three cars in 36 months, is a number I do not enjoy looking at.

The house. In 2018 we bought one. In 2019 we moved in. In the years after, an embarrassing amount of additional money disappeared into "settling in" – the marble we didn't really need, the modular kitchen that came with options I will never use, the home theatre that goes unused for weeks, the appliance upgrades that arrived because somebody at a dinner party mentioned theirs.

The holidays. Every year, slightly nicer. Slightly further. Slightly longer. Slightly more "experiential."

The wardrobe. Slowly upgraded, brand by brand, without any single visible purchase decision. The shirts cost a bit more. The shoes cost a bit more. The watches you're wearing cost a bit more. None of it was a "moment." All of it was a *drift*.

Each one of these, individually, looked perfectly reasonable. Each was justified, internally, by some version of *"we've worked hard, we deserve this, what are we even earning all this for if not to enjoy it."* I am not going to pretend that argument is wrong. It isn't, fully. There is genuine value in enjoying the fruits of your work. The mistake was that I never paused to ask *how much was enough.*

Why the Upgrade Cycle Is Sneakier Than It Looks

The reason this trap is so hard to see while you are inside it is that no single decision feels wrong.

The phone upgrade is ₹1.5 lakh, once every three years. Not a big deal. The watch upgrade is ₹1-2 lakh, once every *couple of years.* Not a big deal. The car upgrade is ₹5-10 lakh of net loss after resale. Not a big deal every couple of years. The marble in the kitchen is ₹2 lakh. Not a big deal. The annual holiday, including the unbudgeted "let's just upgrade to business class" moment at the airport, is ₹3-5 lakh extra over what you'd planned. Not a big deal.

Each one of these is *not a big deal.* The cumulative drag, across a 13-year career, is ₹30-50 lakh that simply did not get invested. Compounded at 12% over the same period, that is a number that would have changed the math of the rest of my life, materially. It is, almost exactly, a fully funded long-horizon goal that quietly never existed.

There is a name for this in behavioural economics: the *hedonic treadmill.* You upgrade, you adjust, the new becomes the baseline, you upgrade again. The pleasure from each new thing lasts shorter than the time it took to earn the money to buy it. By the third or fourth cycle, you barely register the upgrade. By the fifth, the absence of an upgrade feels like a downgrade. The treadmill speeds up, your effective happiness flatlines, and the bank balance that would have funded real freedom keeps not getting built.

I am not the first person to write this. I will not be the last. I am writing it because *knowing* about the hedonic treadmill, in theory, did not stop me from being on it for thirteen years in practice.

The Three Sentences That Started Breaking the Cycle

I cannot pretend I have fully escaped the upgrade habit. I haven't. I still want a new phone every couple of years. I still notice the new watches. I still occasionally talk myself out of a car I shouldn't be looking at.

But somewhere around 2023, three sentences started showing up in my head before any meaningful purchase, and they have, slowly, started doing real work.

Sentence one: *Did I want this six months ago?* If I did, and I have been thinking about it for that long, the desire is real. If I didn't – if it appeared in my head only after I saw a friend's, or a video, or an ad – the desire is the product of a stimulus, not of me. I wait. Most of these desires die quietly within a month. The ones that don't, I revisit.

Sentence two: *What does this upgrade actually replace?* A phone replaces a phone that still works perfectly. A car replaces a car that runs fine. A watch replaces a watch that tells the same time. The honest answer to "what does this replace" is almost always *"a perfectly functional version of itself, plus a feeling."* That feeling has a price tag. I now ask myself if I'd pay the gap as a standalone "feel slightly better about myself" charge. Sometimes yes. More often, no.

Sentence three: What's the experience-equivalent of this? Psychology research is fairly consistent on this: experiences buy more durable happiness than things, especially shared experiences. So before any large material purchase, I now do a quick mental conversion. *This watch is one extraordinary trip. This car upgrade is six months of really nice family weekends.* It does not always change my decision. It changes my decision often enough to matter. Slowly, the centre of gravity has shifted from the things to the bigger goals - my family, my kids, my freedom.

The One Real Behavioural Hack

The single most useful behavioural change I've made on this is not any of the above sentences. It is a much more boring one.

Income jumps go to savings rate first, lifestyle second.

In practice, this means: when a salary goes up by 30%, the savings/SIP rate goes up by 30% the same month, before any new spending decisions are even allowed to be discussed. Not after the upgrade. Not after the holiday. Not after the new car. First. What's left after the upgraded savings rate becomes the new lifestyle budget.

This single rule, applied for the last three or four years, has done more to repair the damage of the previous decade than any individual purchase decision. It does not require willpower in the moment of temptation. It requires one decision, made once, in a calm moment, that quietly hardcodes the good behaviour into the calendar.

If I had run that rule from 2009, I would not have lost a paisa of joy from any of those upgrades. I would have made every one of them, just smaller, slower, and after the savings rate had moved.

What did I learn?

First: *lifestyle inflation is not the lifestyle.* It is the inflation. Enjoying a nicer life as you earn more is fine. The mistake is letting the rate of upgrade exceed the rate of savings. Every income jump is a fork in the road. The wrong fork looks identical to the right fork until you check the bank balance ten years later.

Second: *"I deserve this" is the most expensive sentence in personal finance.* Not because you don't deserve nice things. You do. But that sentence is functionally a permission slip you give yourself to skip the math. The math, when done, almost always allows for some of the upgrade and rejects most of it. The sentence allows for all of it.

Third: *the upgrade you don't notice is the most dangerous one.* Phone upgrades you remember. Wardrobe drift, slightly nicer dinners, the unbudgeted business-class moment at the airport – these don't get logged anywhere in your head. They aggregate silently. The single most useful financial habit I've built is reviewing the credit-card statement *line by line, monthly*, not for fraud, but for the items where I can no longer remember why I bought them.

Fourth, the meta-lesson: *what you are actually buying with most upgrades is not the thing.* It is the feeling of having moved up. That feeling is real, and it is fine to want it. Just price it. Decide how much "moving up" is worth to you per year. Spend exactly that much on it, deliberately. The trouble starts when the feeling-spend is invisible to you and uncapped.

If you take one thing from this chapter – and especially if you are early in your career – let it be this: *every income jump is a savings-rate decision before it is a lifestyle decision.* If you make that one rule yours, you will quietly outrun, over a decade, almost every other piece of personal-finance advice you ever follow.

The cars will still come. The phones will still come. The trips will still happen. They will just happen on top of a balance sheet that is also, finally, growing.

Mistake #14, logged. One more to go.

CHAPTER

15

The Emergency Fund I Didn't Build (And the Two Times It Almost Killed Me)

This is the most boring chapter in the book.

I am announcing that upfront because, if I don't, you will skim the heading, decide you've heard this one before, and skip to the redemption arc. Don't.

For most of my career, I had a working philosophy that sounded sophisticated and was, in retrospect, slightly stupid. It went like this: *every rupee I own should be doing as much work as possible. Cash sitting idle is a sin against compounding. The only money that should be uninvested is exactly enough to cover the next month's expenses.*

So that's how I ran my balance sheet. A thin sliver of cash for the month, and everything else – bonuses, savings, every spare rupee

– pushed into equity, mutual funds, sometimes direct stocks. The *buffer* was minimal on purpose. Idle cash, in my head, was opportunity cost.

This worked. For about a decade. Until two events, four years apart, taught me what was wrong with the philosophy.

The First Wake-Up Call: 2017

When my father passed away, the financial implications hit immediately and from every direction at once.

I needed to fly to Bhopal. I needed to stay there, on and off, for weeks. I needed to wind down a family business with all the messy obligations that come with it. I needed to make payments – sometimes large ones – to settle accounts, with proofs I couldn't always verify. I needed to support family. I needed to cover months of indirect costs that nobody warns you about: travel, lawyers, accountants, paperwork, time off work that wasn't fully paid.

What I had on hand for all of this was the equivalent of one month's monthly expenses, sitting in a bank account.

Everything else was in equity and mutual funds.

Now, the markets in 2017 were not in crisis. So selling wasn't catastrophic in the way 2008 or March 2020 would have been. But selling under emotional duress is its own tax. You sell what you can sell quickly, not what you should sell strategically. You incur exit loads and short-term capital gains because you don't have the time or the head-space to sequence properly. You disrupt SIPs that were quietly compounding. You break your own asset allocation in a moment when your bandwidth to think about asset allocation is exactly zero.

Most importantly: every redemption I had to make was, mentally, salt in the wound. I was already grieving. I was already running on three hours of sleep. And on top of that, I was force-selling the very investments I had spent years building, because I had not built the smaller, simpler thing first – a parked pile of cash.

I came out of 2018 with my equity portfolio noticeably lighter than it should have been. Not because the markets had taken it. Because I had liquidated it under pressure.

I told myself, at the time, next time, I will keep more cash. And then, like every well-intentioned post-crisis resolution, I half-did it for six months and forgot.

Three years later, I was given a much louder reminder.

The Second Wake-Up Call: March 2020

I don't have to remind you what March 2020 felt like, because every reader of this book lived through it.

The Sensex fell from around 41,000 in mid-February to under 26,000 by late March. A 35% drop, in roughly six weeks. The Nifty 50 went from ~12,200 to ~7,600 in the same window. Indian equity wealth lost something like ₹50 lakh crore on paper. Most equity mutual fund portfolios were down 30-40% by month-end.

I was, at the time, at Bank of America. The salary was steady. The job was, by the standards of the moment, secure. So I did not personally need to liquidate anything. The crash was, for me, a paper loss that recovered cleanly through the rest of 2020 and 2021.

But I want you to imagine, for a second, the version of me that did need liquidity in March 2020.

Imagine I had lost the BofA job in early March 2020 (many, many people did, in many sectors). Imagine someone in the family had a medical event in mid-March (many, many families did). Imagine the rent had to be paid, the EMIs had to be paid, the insurance had to be renewed, and the school fees were due – all of which still happened, on schedule, while the world was frozen.

To meet those obligations, I would have had to sell mutual funds at the bottom of a 35% crash. Not 5%. Not 10%. 35%.

The same ₹10 lakh that I had quietly invested over the years would have come out as ₹6.5 lakh, locked in forever. The years of compounding ahead – which we now know would have nearly tripled the same money over the next five years – would have evaporated, because I needed the cash and the cash hadn't been parked anywhere I could reach without breaking the growth engine.

I got lucky in March 2020. The job stayed. The family stayed healthy. The markets recovered. None of the imagined scenarios played out.

But sitting at home through that lockdown, watching the screens turn red day after day, I realised: *the only reason this is "lucky" is because I had built a financial life that depended entirely on luck.*

That was the moment I finally took the boring chapter seriously.

What I Did Differently After March 2020

Within a few months of the worst of the crash, I sat down and rebuilt the cash architecture of my life. Not as an idea. As a number.

The new rule, which I've kept since:

Four months of monthly *household* expenses – not income, not lifestyle, expenses – kept liquid at all times.

A few things in that sentence matter.

Four months, is the realistic minimum for an Indian family in a world where, in a real crisis, finding a comparable job, settling a medical event, or restructuring a business takes longer than people like to admit.

Household expenses, not salary. This is the part most people get wrong. If your salary is ₹3 lakh a month and your actual expenses are ₹1.2 lakh a month, your emergency fund is ₹7.2 lakh, not ₹18 lakh. Pegging the buffer to expenses makes the number affordable to actually build, and it's the right number anyway – what you need protection from is your inability to cover *spending*, not your inability to maintain your *lifestyle*.

Liquid, not "near-liquid." The fund sits across two layers. Roughly two months in a sweep-FD against a savings account – so the cash is one click away. The remaining two months in liquid mutual funds and overnight funds – accessible in 24-48 hours, earning 5-6% a year, low credit risk, low duration risk.

Not earmarked for "alpha." This is the philosophical change. The emergency fund is not trying to generate returns. It is doing a different job entirely: it is the *insulation* that lets the rest of the portfolio compound undisturbed. The yield it earns is incidental. The yield the rest of the portfolio earns because of its *presence* is the actual return.

Why "I'll Just Sell Investments If I Need To" Is the Wrong Plan

Almost every financially literate friend I have, before they had their own version of this wake-up call, defended the "I don't need an emergency fund, I have liquid investments" position. Some of you are, right now, defending it in your head.

It is wrong, and the reason it's wrong is structural, not behavioural.

Emergencies and market drawdowns *correlate*. They don't always happen on the same day, but the conditions that produce one – a recession, a pandemic, a job-losing industry shake-up – disproportionately also produce the other. So the very moment you most need liquidity is, on average, the moment your investments are most depressed. The emergency fund exists to break this correlation. It says *no matter what the market is doing, I have four months to make decisions calmly, and I do not have to participate in the panic.*

There is also a behavioural angle. Even when you can technically sell investments to cover an emergency, doing so during a drawdown is psychologically excruciating. You will hesitate. You will delay. You will make worse decisions about which investments to sell, and in what order. The emergency fund spares you all of that. You spend the cash. You replenish it later, slowly. The growth engine never gets touched.

What did I learn?

First: *the emergency fund is not an investment. It is a permission slip.* It is what allows the rest of the portfolio to do its job without being interrupted by your life. The "low yield" of the cash is the cost of buying that permission. It's one of the cheapest insurance products you'll ever own.

Second: *peg it to expenses, not income.* If you peg it to income, the number gets so big you never start. If you peg it to actual expenses, it becomes achievable in a year or two of disciplined saving. And it is, anyway, the right number.

Third: *build it before you "deserve" it.* I waited until I had been earning a banker's salary for over a decade to take this seriously. Younger me, on a starter salary, needed this fund more, not less. The lower your income, the more catastrophic a single bad month becomes. Emergency fund maturity is an early-career habit, not a late-career one.

Fourth, the meta-lesson: t*he things that look like they're costing you money are often the things saving the most of it.* Idle cash earning 6% looks worse than equity earning 12%. But the day you don't have to sell that 12% portfolio at a 35% drawdown to cover a rent payment, the cash quietly outperformed the equity by an enormous, invisible margin.

I have not had to deeply tap the emergency fund since I built it properly. I hope I never do. But sleeping with it sitting there, especially now that I am building NYVO and not collecting a corporate salary, has changed the texture of every single financial decision I make. The portfolio breathes easier. The market noise matters less. The freedom to take real career risk – including walking away from a job – exists because of it.

That is the entire point.

Mistake #15, logged.

And that – finally, fifteen chapters in – is all of them.

Now for the second half of this book. The part where I tell you what I eventually got right, and what I am building so you don't have to take fifteen years to do the same.

INTERLUDE

A Family Checklist

Before you turn the page into Part II, I want you to put the book down for ten minutes.

This is the only "homework" page in the entire book. There are no scores, no rankings, and no algorithm grading you at the end. There is just a small set of questions that, if you can honestly answer yes to all of them, mean your family is in genuinely good shape – regardless of how much money you've made or what you do for a living.

If the answer to any of them is *no, hmm,* or *I'm not sure,* that is the to-do list for your next quarter.

Take a piece of paper. Or open a Note. Go through them once, with your spouse or partner if you have one, and write the honest answer next to each.

---

1. Do we have personal health insurance, in addition to whatever the employer provides? Cover that follows the family even if the job ends tomorrow. Sized for a serious hospitalisation, not a routine fever.

2. Do I (the primary earner, or both, if both earn) have a pure term insurance policy? Not bundled with a loan. Not a ULIP. Not an "insurance + investment" anything. Pure term. Cover sized at roughly 10–15 times annual income.

3. Is the nominee correct on every account, policy, and folio we own? Bank accounts, mutual funds, demat, EPF (Employee Provident Fund), NPS (National Pension Scheme), every insurance policy. Not the nominee from college. Not the nominee from before the kids were born. The current one.

4. Does my spouse or anyone in the family know where every account, policy, and document is? If something happened to me tomorrow, could they find it all without panic? A single shared list – paper, Google Doc, password manager, anything – is enough.

5. Have I had the conversation with my parents? Where their money is. What insurance they have. Who their CA is. What they would want if something happened. Not as an audit. As a quiet hour over tea.

6. Are our long-horizon goals named and tagged? A "Children's Education" bucket with a date and a target. A "Retirement" bucket with a number. A "Buying a Home" bucket if that is on the horizon. Money that has a name does not get accidentally spent.

7. Do we have an emergency fund of four months of household expenses, parked in liquid instruments? Pegged to expenses, not to income. In a savings account, sweep-FD, or liquid mutual fund. Not in equity. Not in real estate. Liquid.

If you got seven yeses, you are doing better than 95% of urban Indian households I have met. Truly.

If you got four or five, the next quarter has the highest-leverage to-do list of your year. Start with the gaps, not with what's exciting.

If you got fewer than three, please don't panic. None of this is hard. Most of it is one weekend of paperwork. The first step is just admitting the gap exists – which, by reading this list, you have already taken.

When you are done, turn the page. Part II is about what changed for me when I finally started doing all of this myself.

PART II

What I Finally Got Right

CHAPTER

16

Goals, Names, and the Day My Money Started Working for Me

If you've made it this far, congratulations. You have just sat through fifteen chapters of me getting things wrong. Some of them small. Some of them very, very expensive. All of them, in retrospect, completely avoidable if I had known then what I know now.

This is the chapter where I owe you the other side of the ledger.

Because the truth is that, in the middle of all those mistakes, I was also slowly – sometimes accidentally, sometimes deliberately – building a set of habits that, by the time I was 35-36, had quietly delivered me something I had not expected to feel for at least another decade:

Financial freedom.

Not "I-own-a-yacht" freedom. The much more useful kind. The kind where I could sit my wife down, in early 2022, and say, "I want to walk out of Bank of America. I don't want to draw a salary for a few years. I want to build something of our own." And she could look at the spreadsheet, take a long breath, and say, "Okay. Let's do it."

That conversation was possible because of the things in this chapter. Not the mistakes. The things I – we – slowly got right.

There are six of them. None of them are clever. All of them are repeatable. If I could bundle them into a single envelope and hand them to 22-year-old me, the timeline of my life would have looked very different. Maybe yours can.

1. The Salary-Day Rule: Save First, Spend Second

For the first ten years of my career, the order of operations on salary day looked like this:

1. Salary credits to bank account.
2. Spend through the month.
3. Whatever is left at the end of the month – if anything is left – moves to savings or investments. (Yes, even with the auto-SIPs running, the behavioural trap is in what happens to everything outside the auto-SIP.)

This is, unfortunately, the order of operations that most Indian salaried professionals run by default. It is also, mathematically, the worst possible order. Because what's left at the end of the month is, almost without exception, *less than you intended and less than you needed.* Every "small" expense, every dinner, every Amazon impulse, every "we deserve this" moment quietly eats into the residual. And the residual is what you were supposed to be saving.

Somewhere in 2019 or so, I flipped the order. The new sequence:

1. Salary credits to bank account.
2. *Same day or next day,* a fixed amount – defined in advance – sweeps out automatically into investments. SIPs. Lump-sum mutual fund purchases. Whatever the plan said.
3. Whatever is left becomes the actual budget for the month. (spent from another bank account.)

That's it. That's the whole rule.

The technical version of this is "pay yourself first." The real-world version of it is the *discipline of treating savings as a non-negotiable first call on income, the way rent is a first call.* You wouldn't say "I'll pay rent if there's anything left at the end of the month." Your savings deserve the same hierarchy.

A practical detail that helped me: when I was busy– I would sometimes not have time to make the proper investment moves on salary day. So I built a 30-second fallback. If I couldn't decide what to do with the surplus that day, the surplus would go *straight into a fixed deposit* the same evening, even if it earned a sub-optimal 5-6%. The point was not to leave it sitting in the savings account, where it would silently get spent. Better to have ₹50,000 in an FD I'd later move into equity than ₹50,000 in a current account that disappears into "I don't quite remember where."

The 30-second rule has done more for my net worth than any single investment decision I've ever made.

2. Name Every Bucket

Until about five or six years ago, my net worth lived in a single mental category called *"my investments."* Equity, mutual funds, the home, the EPF, the savings – one undifferentiated pile. I knew the total. I did not know what any of it was for.

This was, I now realise, the single biggest reason for many of the mistakes in the first half of this book. Money that has no name has no purpose. Money that has no purpose gets allocated badly, withdrawn at the wrong moments, and quietly reassigned to whatever the next emergency or temptation happens to be.

Today, my investments are not "investments" anymore. They are *named pots,* each with a job, an owner, and a date.

- **Nysha Startup Fund** – for our daughter, target date roughly 2039. Equity-heavy, long-horizon, untouchable.
- **Neel Education Fund** – for our son, target date roughly 2044. Same shape, longer horizon.
- **Retirement Fund** – for Nilisha and me, target date roughly 2050. Long-horizon equity tilt with a debt sleeve.
- **Emergency Fund** – four months of expenses, liquid.
- **Lifestyle Fund** – flexible cash for the next 12-24 months of larger family decisions and the occasional planned indulgence. Some equity, some debt.
- **NYVO Runway Fund** – what's keeping me alive while I build a company without a salary.

Each of these has its own folio. Each has its own asset allocation. Each has its own contribution. Each has a target amount and a target date written next to it on a single sheet of paper that lives, literally, in a drawer in my home office.

The act of naming has done two things to my behaviour that no other discipline has matched.

First, *I do not touch named money.* I cannot bring myself to dip into the Nysha Startup Fund because something looked tempting on a Saturday. The act of having to think *"would I withdraw from Nysha's bucket for this?"* is, by itself, the cleanest filter on bad spending decisions I have ever installed. It is shame-driven, and shame, channeled correctly, is one of the most effective behavioural tools available to a human being managing money.

Second, *I make better allocation decisions for each bucket because the time horizon is explicit.* Nysha's bucket has a 14-year horizon. So it's almost entirely equity. The Family Buffer has a 1-2 year horizon. So it's almost entirely safe investments. Without naming, the same money would have sat in the same average asset allocation, generating worse results in both directions.

If you do one thing after reading this book, do this. Not because it's clever. Because it's the change that moves the most levers at once.

3. Buy Real Protection Before Anything Else - the True Defence Layer

Chapters 6 (health insurance), 7 (term insurance bundled with home loan), and 15 (emergency fund) all converge here, so I'll keep this short.

Protection comes before growth. Insurance comes before investing. Survival comes before returns.

This is not a sentence you'll see on the cover of any glossy mutual fund brochure, because the people who sell mutual funds make their money on AUM, not on insulation. But it is the single most important hierarchy in personal finance, and once I internalised it, the architecture of our family's money got much simpler.

The shape of the protection layer for us today:

- **Comprehensive personal health insurance,** bought for the whole family – including parents, including the kids on day 91. Sufficient base cover (₹15-25 lakh per adult), no co-pay, no room rent limit, no sub-limits.
- **Pure term insurance for me** – 15x annual income, fixed-cover, level-premium, pure protection.
- **Four-month emergency fund** in liquid instruments.

This entire layer costs us less, annually, than a few weeks of household groceries. It is, by miles, the highest-ROI spending we do.

If you are early in your career and you have to choose between starting your SIP and buying real protection – buy the protection first. The compounding will catch up. The protection cannot be retroactively bought after the fact.

4. Investing on Fundamentals, Not Tips

This one took the longest to learn. Chapters 3 (mutual funds by past returns), 5 (crypto), and 12 (the stock-strategy carnival) are all about different versions of the same mistake: *investing on signals other than fundamentals.*

What changed, eventually, was that I forced myself to articulate, in one paragraph, why I was buying anything before I bought it. Not a tip. Not a screenshot from a Twitter thread. Not a smallcase tagline. *Why.*

Once you make yourself write the why, two things happen.

First, you discover that you can't write a why for at least two-thirds of the things you would have otherwise bought. You don't actually have a thesis on Polygon vs Ethereum. You don't actually understand what makes one mid-cap fund different from another. You don't actually know what business this stock is in. The act of writing the why exposes the missing why, and you skip the buy.

Second, when you can write the why, you make it bigger. Conviction, properly grounded, deserves position size. Most of the alpha I've made in the last two years has come from a handful of positions where I had a genuine thesis and sized accordingly. Most of the losses in the years before came from a hundred positions where I had no thesis and sized recklessly.

Tips are noise. Influencer takes are noise. Basket and theme products are noise. Past returns are noise. Why is the only signal that matters, and you have to write it down before you act, because if you write it after, you'll just rationalise.

5. Define Goals, Dreams, and Nightmares – In That Order

Here is a mental model I picked up somewhere in the last few years that has, more than anything else, organised my financial brain. It splits everything money is for into three honest categories.

Goals are the things you *will* need money for, with high probability and known timing. Children's education. Retirement. A home.

Family responsibilities. These are not aspirations. They are obligations. Goals need *structure*, not hope.

Dreams are the things you'd love to have but life will be fine without. A nicer car. A long sabbatical. Travel. Starting a business. A second home. These give life its meaning, but they are negotiable. Dreams should be funded after goals, with an explicit "dream bucket" you can spend without guilt because the goals are already covered.

Nightmares are the things that will destroy your finances if they happen and you're not prepared. Hospitalisation. Critical illness. Untimely death. A family member's medical event. Sudden loss of income. These don't just take money. They take *momentum*. Nightmares need to be insured against first, not last.

Most personal finance advice in India focuses obsessively on Dreams (high returns! the next multibagger!) and ignores both Goals (boring) and Nightmares (depressing). The reason every single chapter in the first half of this book is a chapter is that I, too, focused on Dreams while leaving Goals under-funded and Nightmares uninsured.

Once I started running the family's money in this order – *Nightmares first, Goals second, Dreams third* – almost every individual financial decision became easier. Should I buy this thing? *Have we covered all Nightmares? Are all Goals on track? If yes, the Dream bucket is fair game. If no, this can wait.*

6. Stop Chasing Every Upgrade

Chapter 14 (The Upgrade Cycle) covered this in detail, so I'll keep it brief here. The single sentence that changed everything:

Income jumps go to savings rate first, lifestyle second.

Every salary increment, every bonus, every promotion – the first move is to bump the savings, not to bump the lifestyle. Whatever's left after the upgraded savings rate becomes the new spending budget. The upgrades still happen, just smaller, slower, more deliberate, and on top of a savings rate that's also growing.

This single rule, applied for the last few years, has done more to repair the damage of the previous decade than any other behavioural change.

What "Financial Freedom at 36" Actually Means

I want to be precise about this phrase, because it's used too loosely on the internet and I don't want it to sound like I'm describing something it isn't.

I am not retired. I work harder now, on NYVO, than I did at any point at Bank of America or at slice. The hours are longer. The stress is, in many ways, more constant. This is not financial *retirement*. It is financial *freedom*, which is a different thing.

What it concretely means, for our family, is this:

- All Nightmares are covered. If any one of them happens tomorrow, the family's standard of living does not change.
- All Goals are on track. The Nysha Startup Fund, the Neel Education Fund, and the Retirement Fund are funded at trajectories that, if I never put another rupee into them, would still meet their targets.
- The Emergency Fund and the Lifestyle / Dream Funds are fully topped up, giving us 24+ months of runway without touching anything else.

- Our monthly expenses are met by passive income – rental, debt yield, fund yield – plus my wife's salary, without requiring me to draw one of my own.

That last bullet is the operational definition. *Our family lives without me having to earn a paycheck.* The investing returns and the passive income cover the burn. The actively-earned salary, if any, is on top of that.

This is what gave me the courage to walk out of BofA in February 2022, then out of slice in 2025, and bet the next phase of my life on building NYVO. It is not luck. It is not the bonus. It is the slow, deliberate stacking of these six habits over a few years, on top of the thirteen years of mistakes that taught me they were necessary.

If I had started building these habits at 24 instead of 34, I would have been free at 30, not 36.

If you start building them today, you can be free earlier than I was.

That, in a sentence, is the entire promise of the back half of this book – and the entire reason for the chapter that follows.

PART III

What We're Building

NYVO stands for New Voice.

CHAPTER

17

Why I Started NYVO Money

I want to begin this last chapter by being honest about what it is, and what it isn't.

It isn't a sales pitch. If you've made it through fifteen chapters of mistakes and a chapter of redemption, you've already given me far more of your time than any product page deserves. I am not going to use the closing pages of this book to ask you to download an app.

What this chapter is, is a story about the Indian household.

About what happens to it when it tries to navigate money on its own. About why something is broken in a country where, on paper, more financial products are available to more people than ever before – and yet, the average Indian family still ends up making the same fifteen mistakes I made.

NYVO is the thing my co-founder Kshitij and I are building because of that brokenness. But the brokenness is the point of this chapter. NYVO is one possible answer to it.

The Indian Family Money Problem

Let me describe a household. You will recognise it, because it is some version of every household I have grown up in or married into or worked alongside.

A husband and wife in their early-to-mid thirties. One or two kids. Both parents alive, retired or close to it. A mortgage, or aspirations of one. A car. School fees that are real money. A monthly SIP, started two years ago because somebody at work mentioned they should. A LIC policy from 2008 that the husband doesn't fully remember signing. A health policy through the employer. A second health policy somebody's uncle insisted they buy. An EPF account each. Maybe a PPF. Maybe a mutual fund or three, picked at different times for different reasons that nobody can now reconstruct.

This household, on paper, is doing many of the right things. Saving. Investing. Insured. Earning well.

If you ask either spouse – and I have asked many of them – *"how much money do you need for your daughter's college?"* They don't know.

"Are you on track?" They don't know.

"What is your retirement number?" They don't know.

"What happens to the family's monthly expenses if one income disappears tomorrow?" They don't know.

"What's the cover on your term plan, and is it enough?" They don't know – and roughly half the time, they don't have a term plan at all.

"Who is the nominee on each of your accounts?" Awkward silence.

These are not unintelligent people. Many of them are doctors, engineers, lawyers, founders, bankers – people who would, in their professional lives, never tolerate this level of ambiguity about anything else they were responsible for. But about the money that determines whether their child can study where they want to study, whether their parents will be looked after with dignity, whether their family will be okay if life takes a sudden turn – they have no clear picture. They have products. They do not have a plan.

That gap, between the pile of products the average Indian family owns and the simple plan they should have, is the entire problem we are trying to solve.

Why the Gap Exists

The gap is not the family's fault.

The Indian financial services industry, for all its size and sophistication, has organised itself around a single, very efficient business model: *sell products, collect commissions, move on.* The agent who sold your father the LIC policy in 2003 wasn't paid to ask whether it was the right product for him. He was paid for the sale. The relationship manager who calls you about a "new fund offer" isn't trained to evaluate whether you need it. He has a target for the quarter. The online insurance marketplace that recommended a ULIP to a banker, who should have known better, isn't a neutral platform. It is a sales channel with better UI.

This is not a moral failure of the people involved. Most of them are doing their jobs as the system has structured them. The failure is structural. The incentives at every layer push *product over plan, commission over suitability, short-term sale over long-term outcome.*

The result is what I have come to call **confident misinformation**. The Indian family today is not short of financial information. They are *drowning* in it – Twitter threads, Instagram reels, Telegram tip channels, finfluencers, brokers, insurance agents, RM calls, well-meaning relatives, and a brother-in-law who is "doing F&O these days." All of these voices speak with enormous confidence. Almost none of them are accountable for what happens after you take their advice.

There is a deep, troubling pattern in this. The more confident the voice, the further it tends to be from the truth. The most useful financial advice rarely sounds exciting. It almost never goes viral. The voices that go viral are exactly the ones an honest planner would tell you to avoid.

The 0.5% Problem

There is a parallel, slightly hidden, version of this story that is worth naming.

In India today, the top 0.5% of households – the ultra-HNI (High Net Worth Individuals) segment – get genuinely good financial advice. Real planners. Discretionary portfolio managers. Tax planners. Estate planners. Family office structures. Multi-generational thinking.

This advice exists, and it is excellent, *because* the chunky portfolios involved make it economically rational for the advisor to invest the time. A planner who manages ₹50 crore for a family can afford to spend twenty hours a quarter understanding that family. The fees justify the depth.

For the other 99.5% of Indian households, the same depth of advice does not exist – not because the families don't deserve it, but because the unit economics don't work in the traditional model. A planner cannot spend twenty quarterly hours on a ₹10 lakh portfolio. So that family gets, instead, a salesperson with a brochure. The same family that makes the same fifteen mistakes I made, and pays the same compounding price for them.

This is the real inequity in Indian personal finance. The wealthy get *advice*. Everyone else gets *products*.

That gap – between the planning the top 0.5% receive and the salesmanship everyone else receives – is the gap NYVO is built to close.

What "Good Advice" Actually Looks Like

Before I describe what we're building, let me describe what good advice looks like to me, after twenty years of receiving every other kind.

Good advice **starts with the family, not the product.** It begins with a conversation about goals, dreams, and nightmares (which I covered in the previous chapter, and which the framework on page 115 from our work breaks down further). It maps the family's actual life – the children, the parents, the income shape, the obligations – before anything called a "product" is even discussed.

Good advice **is honest about the limits of investing.** It accepts that the highest-leverage moves in personal finance are usually the boring, defensive ones – health insurance, term insurance, an emergency fund, a goal-tagged SIP – and it sets these up *before* it tries to chase any return.

Good advice **does not earn its money from what it sells you.** It earns its money from the *time and judgement* it invests in your situation. Fee-only, transparent, repeating, accountable.

Good advice **brings discipline, not drama.** It doesn't get excited about the latest small-cap. It doesn't urgently need you to "act today." It doesn't replace itself with a new shiny thing every quarter. The same plan, applied for ten years, will outperform almost any clever rotation. The advisor's job is to help you stay on it.

Good advice **respects your time.** It doesn't call you twenty times because you checked a price. It doesn't spam your WhatsApp. It doesn't sell your phone number to three other entities. It quietly does its job and gets out of your way.

Almost none of these things describe the experience of an average Indian family interacting with the financial services industry today.

What We Are Trying to Be

NYVO Money is, in the simplest possible language, an attempt to make *real* financial planning available to the 99.5% of Indian households who today do not get it.

It is not a sales channel or a recommendation engine attached to a commission funnel. It is a *plan-first* companion that begins with your goals, names your buckets, builds the protection layer that should have been there from day one, and walks you through the discipline of building wealth over a lifetime – without us earning anything from any specific investment product you happen to buy as a result.

The frame we work with is the one I shared in the previous chapter:

Goals (the things you will need money for, on a known timeline),

Dreams (the things that give life its meaning, funded after Goals), and

Nightmares (the things that, if uninsured, take both your wealth and your momentum). Get those three buckets right, in that order, and almost everything else takes care of itself.

There is no exotic alpha promise. There is no "best fund of the year" pitch. There is no magic. There is the slow, structured, named application of the things I should have done from the day I started earning, made available to families who deserve to have them done properly without paying ultra-HNI fees for the privilege.

What we want to do, in one sentence, is to make your money stress-free.

The Story Behind the Name

I owe you a small footnote, because the name has a story I am quietly proud of.

Our family is built on the letter N.

My wife, **Nilisha** – who has carried me through every one of these mistakes and the smarter half of every right decision.

Our daughter, **Nysha** – born October 2019, currently the chief opinion-haver in the household.

Our son, **Neel** – born 2024, currently the chief opinion-needer.

When Kshitij and I were thinking of names for what we were building, I knew it had to start with N. Whatever we were building was, in a real sense, the third child Nilisha and I were going to raise. It deserved the same letter as the other two.

NYVO stands for *New Voice.*

We picked it because, more than anything else, that's what we want to be in the lives of the families we work with – *a new voice* in a room that, for too long, has been dominated by salespeople, influencers, and well-meaning relatives who don't actually know what they're talking about. A voice that speaks honestly. A voice that has no incentive to mis-sell. A voice that remembers, every day, that on the other side of every "portfolio" is a family with a child's college, a parent's old age, and a thousand small dreams that money is supposed to make possible.

That is what we are trying to be. We will not always get it right. But the intent is clean, and the intent is the part the industry has been missing for decades.

The Last Word

I started writing this book as a marketing exercise for the company. Long-form content, the modern playbook said. Build trust through honesty. Show your scars.

Somewhere in the middle of writing it – probably around Chapter 10, when I had to actually sit with what I had not done for my parents – it stopped being a marketing exercise. It became a kind of public reckoning. A chance to write down, in one place, the version of the conversation I wish someone had had with 22-year-old me. The conversation almost no Indian young person gets to have with anyone, because the people closest to them are awkward about money, and the people farthest from them have something to sell.

If even one chapter in this book makes you do one thing differently – buy the term plan, name a fund, have the conversation with your parents, kill the ULIP, sit with a fee-only planner – I will consider this book paisa vasool.

If it makes you curious about NYVO, our doors are open. If it doesn't, that is also fine. The book exists either way. The mistakes are real either way. The fifteen years are not coming back, for me or for you.

What you do with the next fifteen, however, are still entirely yours to decide.

That decision, by the way, is the entire game. Almost everything important in personal finance comes down to a small number of structural choices, made early, and stuck with through every cycle of noise. Simple changes. Clear thinking. Consistent discipline. Over time, they create extraordinary value. Not instantly. But inevitably.

I'd love to hear from you, however you found this book. My email is **harsh@nyvo.in**. I read everything that comes in. Tell me which chapter hit, which one you wish I'd written better, which mistake you've made that I haven't. If you want to try what we're building, the door is at **https://nyvo.money**, and there is no salesperson on the other side of it.

Thank you for reading. Thank you for trusting me with the kind of attention you don't owe a stranger.

Now – go check your nominees, name a fund, and call your parents.

– Harsh

www.ingramcontent.com/pod-product-compliance
Lightning Source LLC
Chambersburg PA
CBHW020240250926
51848CB00007BA/514
9789360700522